CW01655762

Designed, typeset, printed and published by
D. W. Jones (Printers) Ltd. 2000.

First Edition printed in Great Britain in June 2000
by D.W.Jones (Printers) Ltd.
Empire Buildings, Beverley Street, Port Talbot, SA13 1DY

ISBN 0-9532038-3-2

CONTENTS

	League Sponsors	Page 5
	Officers of the League	Page 6
	Why and How this Book was Written	Page 7
	Foreword	Page 8
Chapter 1	The Early Years	Page 10
Chapter 2	The Forties	Page 26
Chapter 3	The Fifties	Page 40
Chapter 4	The Sixties	Page 64
Chapter 5	The Seventies	Page 84
Chapter 6	The Eighties	Page 97
Chapter 7	The Nineties	Page 115
Chapter 8	The Referees Society	Page 140
Chapter 9	Six-a-side Competition	Page 146
Chapter 10	One Hundred Years of Memories	Page 149
Chapter 11	A Tribute to Colin Ashford	Page 158
Chapter 12	League and International Players	Page 160
Chapter 13	Past Officers of the League	Page 162

PIC-UP SPARES LTD.

OFFICIAL SPONSORS TO THE SWANSEA SENIOR ASSOCIATION FOOTBALL LEAGUE.

T. SWAIN

A. HUGHES

B. SOMERVILLE

Pic-Up Spares Ltd., are proud to be associated with the Swansea Senior Association Football League, having been their official sponsors since 1992. It has been a very exciting partnership and one that the Company hopes will continue for years to come.

We as a Company have recently celebrated our 25 years in business, a large contributing factor in our success has been the teamwork of both Directors and Staff. Our Company has a loyal and dedicated team, and we are sure that it is this such teamwork that has seen the Swansea League develop and flourish to provide football for the local population for the past 100 years.

All three Directors have a very close affinity to the League for many years. Tim and Brendan have both given valuable service as players and supporters of the Winch Wen and Port Tennant Colts clubs respectively, whilst Alan has been an avid supporter of local soccer for most of his life.

Pic-Up Spares are very proud to sponsor the League and it gives added pleasure to be associated with them during this landmark Centenary celebration. We congratulate every one with the Swansea League and look forward with anticipation to the coming season.

Tim Swain.
Brendan Somerville.
Alan Hughes.

SWANSEA SENIOR ASSOCIATION FOOTBALL LEAGUE.

(Sponsored by Pic-Up Spares Ltd.)

CENTENARY SEASON 2000-2001
OFFICERS OF THE LEAGUE

President: L. G. DAVIES.

Chairman: T. S. HAMMETT **Vice Chairman:** S. J. BEASLEY

Secretary: L. S. EVANS **Treasurer:** S. L. McDONALD

Asst. Sec: V. J. NEDIN **Fixture Sec:** D. HABBERFIELD

Admin. Sec: MISS S. ASHFORD

Senior Life Members: Messrs. J. Budge, B. J. Bidder, T. M. Bailey, C. C. Price.

Life Members: Messrs. J. Cohen, K. Evans, L. G. Davies, L. Morgan, L. Buckland, D. Savage, J. Hurley.

Vice Presidents: Messrs. R. Paddison, C. D. Thomas, N. Tucker J. Carter.

Executive Committee: Messrs. S. Draper, G. Gambule, D. Bennett, Norman, D. Edwards, B. Cotton, K. Nelson, M. Jones, J. Evans, K. Price, W. Maunder, C. Parkin, G. Stockton.

Referees Repres.: T. G. East.

Hon. Vice-Pres.: Messrs. R. A. Kent, R. Anderson.

WHY AND HOW THIS BOOK WAS WRITTEN.

It was after Colin Ashford's death in 1996, that his widow Jean said that it was sad that no one had ever attempted to put together the history of the League. She suggested that with the forthcoming '100 years of the League' celebration in the year 2000-2001, perhaps it would be possible to produce a brochure or book, illustrating the wonderful history of this great League. At the time it seemed an improbable task, when the work eventually started it was felt by many that it was more an impossible task.

Many League members felt that producing such a work would be a fitting tribute to Colin, they were mindful of the time and dedication that he had given to the League over many years. It was felt that if it was at all possible then we should try to go along with Jean's wishes.

What the League have attempted to do is to produce a fair and neutral detail of its history, one hopes that this book will evoke memories for many people, not just those who have participated in this great League, but for their families and friends, and even the sporting public of Swansea as a whole.

The completion of this work would have been a lot more difficult without the loyalty and dedication of Colin's daughter Simone, apart from a lot of hands on work, she has been the inspiration behind the venture.

The League hope that the completed work would have met with Colin's approval. It is a work that is dedicated to Jean and Simone, in memory of his dedicated service to the Swansea Senior League.

FOREWORD

I am very pleased to be given the opportunity to write this foreword for the Swansea Senior League's 100th Anniversary Brochure. For an organisation to have kept going for one hundred years is an excellent achievement and may I take this opportunity to congratulate all those who are involved with the Swansea Senior League.

I am aware that during this time the Swansea League has got stronger and stronger and is now one of the largest Saturday leagues in England and Wales. My family have been associated with the Swansea league for over half its life and whilst I have been at various times Secretary, Player, Referee and Trainer, my father refereed in the Swansea League after the second world war. The Swansea League like a lot of organisations has relied upon the voluntary contribution and goodwill of very many people. There are people who have given up their time to be managers, club secretaries and committee members of both clubs and the Swansea League Management Committee itself. We, the people of Swansea owe a debt of gratitude to those people who have ensured that the league has continued and been well run over the last 100 years.

There must be tens of thousands of people who have enjoyed playing soccer in the Swansea senior league. I would like to wish Swansea Senior League every success in both its centenary year and the next hundred years.

M. J. HEDGES,
LEADER,
City and County of Swansea.

ACKNOWLEDGEMENT

As anyone who has attempted to carry out such a work will realise, only when the basic history and records are being kept, then it becomes possible to piece together and produce a fairly comprehensive record. We as a League, for all our standing and virtue, had no such records, for all the remarkable administrators the League have been fortunate to have over the years, records and data have never been kept. It was also unfortunate that the League has lost a lot of its old stalwarts over the past few years, members with very long service, who on their passing, took with them a wealth of knowledge of the Swansea League over the years.

Thanks initially go to Dr. J. R. Alban, former City Archivist, who kindly took the time to outline our requirements and to furnish some very early knowledge. It was his enthusiasm at the outset that gave the push to carry on the work. The League are also very grateful to the South Wales Evening Post for all their help in this project. Mr. George Edwards and his staff have been incredibly supportive, special thanks go to Mr. Edwards, Barbara Powell, Liam O'Sullivan, David Roberts, Gareth Vincent and someone who has been a great friend and supporter of the Senior League for many years, Mr. David Evans. David has provided outstanding support for local football, and has always been available to promote the League, his help in producing this work has been invaluable.

The League would also like to point out that a large percentage of the photographs in this edition are by "COURTESY OF THE SOUTH WALES EVENING POST".

Another great help has been the efforts of Brian Lile, a former player in the Senior League who now resides in Aberystwyth, he again passed on information he had accumulated in his research of the early years of football in the Swansea area. To all those who contributed in any small way, whether by lending photographs, cuttings or such material, the League is greatly indebted. In this respect no praise is too high for the efforts of Mr. Billy Davies of Hafod Brotherhood. Billy has been an enormous help to this venture, his enthusiasm and help has been invaluable.

The Swansea Senior League has become an institution over the years. Wherever one may be, it is inevitable that the subject will turn to football. More often than not, it is the local league that is under discussion. The League has been fortunate to have had not only great administrators, but to have produced many fine clubs, players and club officials. It is a League that is the envy of many. The league would like to put on record its deepest thanks for the clubs, players, officials and supporters that have graced this League for 100 years. Long may it continue.

We have been fortunate to have been able to secure the Services of D. W. Jones Ltd., to produce our centenary book. They have been a tremendous help in all aspects of the work and helped and guided us through what could have proved a minefield. No praise is high enough for both John Ganz and Anthony Evans, they were both prepared to sit and listen to our needs and problems. In their case nothing was a problem and they gave us so much confidence.

Special thanks also go to Mrs. Catriona Nedin, wife of the League Assistant Secretary, she has spent many long hours reading, checking and correcting, an arduous but vitally important part of the project.

Finally, it must be recorded that without the help and backing of our sponsors, Pic-Up Spares Ltd., then this venture would not have reached the printers. They have not only provided the financial backing, but have been fully supportive and as keen as the League to complete the work. We cannot thank them enough for their support.

CHAPTER 1 - THE EARLY YEARS

Although history reveals that football, both soccer and rugby, had been played for perhaps centuries, it was not until around the 1840's that these games were beginning to be played on a more organised level. It was around this time that such games, which had until then been played mostly by local peasant youths were now beginning to be organised in the local schools and Public Schools. Up until this time no one had really played either code to specified laws. With the ever growing stature of both codes it became inevitable that newly codified rules would be introduced.

With these new rules came a new generation of players, farmers and company employers were now keen to encourage their workers to take up the sport as an outlet for their leisure time. At the same time many clergymen took the opportunity to use the sport as a means of enticing young players to the church or chapels with matches between the local congregations becoming a regular feature.

Organised soccer teams came into being under the umbrella of the landowners, industrialists and headmasters. The Town at the time was ever expanding, with an active port and heavy industry being set up meant an influx of workers and the inevitable increase in population.

It became obvious that both codes would further develop in this area. The Town (as it was then) had its first soccer team by 1872 with, both the Towns soccer and rugby teams playing their matches at the St. Helens ground. Within a few short years the club switched entirely to the fifteen man code. The field at St. Helens was bought and it was then that the Swansea Football and Cricket club came into existence.

Although during this period rugby was the areas most popular sport, there was constantly a lot of soccer being played in the Town. It would be true however to say that as far as Wales was concerned soccer was almost exclusively a game belonging to the North. J. R. Morgan (Swansea) became the first South Walian to appear for the national side when he played against Scotland in 1879, and to show the emergence of the game in the South of the country some 7,000 spectators turned up at St. Helens to see Wales play Ireland in 1884.

Football in north of Wales had grown particularly strong in the 1870's. Teams there were able to bring in players with experience from the heavily industrialised Merseyside area, with a lot of these players having been attracted to the area to seek employment. There were many fine teams in North Wales at the time, none more so than the Wrexham town side who were almost invincible in Welsh soccer at the turn of the century. They won the inaugural Welsh Cup in 1877, where all the entrants were North Wales clubs apart from a Swansea eleven, they would go on and dominate this competition for many years.

It was in 1898 that perhaps one of the first organised leagues in the South Wales area was formed. The Swansea Schools League was created with the majority of their league matches being played at the Vetch Field (the then home of local amateur side Swansea Villa), the games being played regularly on Saturdays between the hours of 10.00 am and 3.30 pm. Other pitches used at the time included the Recreation Ground and the Intermediate School at Mount Pleasant.

At the turn of the century the Football Association of Wales would boast of 69 clubs, which were mostly based in North and Mid Wales. The Association also reported at the time that soccer in the South Wales area was developing fast and many more clubs were being formed.

It was inevitable that organised football would have to come and in 1901 the Swansea Junior League took on the responsibility for the start of the first organised football league in the Swansea area, this League being set up by a number of junior clubs in the Town. The Chairman of this new League was a Mr. Jeff Walters who incidentally was one of only two referees who were available to officiate, whilst the Secretary appointed was a Mr. Charles Jenkins. Mr. Jenkins was Secretary of the League since its inception in 1901 and held the position until season 1922 when he became the first Secretary of the newly formed West Wales Football Association. He was rightly regarded as one of the foremost administrators of the Association code in the Western area and served the Association until his death in 1938. In those early days, Mr. Jenkins was greatly assisted by Mr. S. B. Williams, who later went on to become Secretary of Swansea Town A. F. C. and then took over as Secretary of the West Wales F. A. after relinquishing his post at the Vetch Field in 1946. Mr. Williams continued in this position up until his death in 1961. Local football has a lot to thank these two giants for their work in establishing such a strong Association in the Swansea area.

In the season of 1903-04, such was the progress of local football, that a Senior division of clubs was formed and in season 1905-06 the word 'District' was added to the name of the League. This was not surprising when such teams as Briton Ferry, Ton Pentre, Llanelly, Carmarthen Training College, Neath, Pontardawe, and Aberdare were in competition, with quite a few of these teams having progressed to Welsh League and League of Wales status. Surprisingly the League's administration does not hold records of the early years but research of the Cambrian Leader newspapers at the Swansea Museum shows the following fixture list for the Swansea & District League for September 1906:-

Morriston	v	Glanbrydan	at	Morriston
Swansea Town	v	Llanelly		Vetch Field
East Side	v	Danygraig		Victoria Park
Manselton	v	St. Paul's		Plasmarl
Swansea Vale	v	Mumbles Albion		Mumbles
Port Talbot	v	Mond Nickel		Port Talbot
York Place	v	St. Mary's		Victoria Park
Pontardawe	v	Brecon		Pontardawe
Sketty	v	Clydach		Hendrefoilan
East Side	v	Skewen		Kilvey Hill.

Records show that in the mid 1890's, soccer became more organised and a League was set up in 1896. This league is not to be confused with the Swansea & District League which officially started in 1901. The champions of this early league for the first three years were Brynmill, other teams in this division included East Side, St. Paul's (Landore), Briton Ferry, St. Marks, Temple Wanderers and Swansea Seconds. By season 1899-1900, the league would include Morriston, Mount Pleasant, and Swansea Wanderers, the champions in this season were Pontardawe who were run by the industrialist C. F. Gilbertson.

At the start of the 1901-1902 season, the inaugural season of the Swansea & District League, the Post reported that 'the Association game is making great headway among the young athletes of the Town at the expense of the rugby game' which it described as being in a 'lugubrious condition'. Mr. Gilbertson's Pontardawe team, fresh from their single season in the higher realms of the South Wales League won the initial championship. The League included the following teams:- Brynmill, Priorton Villa, East Side, Briton Ferry, and the two church teams, St. Andrews and Mount Pleasant.

It is strange to record that with the ever expanding stature of the association code in the Swansea area at this time, no reference of local soccer or league tables appeared in the local press until season 1906. It is known however, that by season 1903-04, East Side, 'the St. Thomas men' - were 'generally recognised as the best exponents of the soccer code in the area'. This lack of coverage by the press, makes it very difficult to portray a true record of the League and its teams. What is known is that more

East Side Association Football Club, (Champions Swansea and District Junior League). SEASON 1902-1903 Matches played 20. Won 20. Goals for 90. Against 10.
T. Williams, (Sec). J. Fisher, (Committee). T. Hardee. A. Margetts. S. L. Francis. T. Bennett. A. Young. F. Nedin. J. Evans. D. John. John, (Committee). D. R. Gent. C. James. H. Kift, (Capt). T. Owen. T. Williams, (Vice-Capt). W. Kift. A. Morgan. S. Leyshon. T. Norman. C. ROBERTS, Photo. Castle Street, SWANSEA.

teams were being formed and would become part of the League, with names including Victoria, White Rose, St. James, St. Pauls, Siloh, Brunswick Mission, Belgrave, Clifton, Danygraig and Knap Lwyd.

It was on the 24th September 1906, when the Post announced:

> It is proposed to form a strong senior association team for Swansea, and for this purpose a meeting has been convened at 'Crayford', 82 St. Helens Road for Tuesday evening (25th) at 8.00 p.m., when Mr. W. Rundle will act as secretary pro tem.

The club they formed was Swansea Town, amateur precursors of the professional club of the same name. Within three-and-a-half years the club would fold, but for most of the their short existence they were the best team in the neighbourhood, winning the Swansea & District League in 1907 and 1908, and, with East Side, entering the South Wales Cup as the first Western representatives since Pontardawe eight years earlier. It would be five years later, in 1912, when the official Swansea Town team would become a professional, truly representative side when they joined the Southern League.

On the 12th January 1907, the Swansea & District League officials were requested to hold a meeting with the South Wales & Monmouthshire F.A., who at the time were the governing body of football in the South Wales area. This body in turn were affiliated to the Welsh F. A.. After lengthy discussion and debate it was decided that the Swansea & District League, taking into consideration the ever increasing growth of football in the South Wales area, would now become an affiliated member of the South Wales & Monmouthshire F. A.. This affiliation would last until season 1922, when the Welsh F. A. decided that with the spread of football in the South, a new body, the West Wales Football Association would come into operation.

It was not until the 1906/1907 season that championship and cup records were officially kept. It was at the District League's annual supper in May 1907, that one of the Towns most prominent players, Milbourne Williams, spoke of the excellent expositions of the 'soccer code' which were given locally. He also suggested that nets should be used for the following season and that pitches should be roped in. Mr. Williams also echoed the sentiments of the Chairman in that trophies should be put up for competition. He declared himself willing to be a subscriber to the extent of one guinea.

It was also during this season that the first report of ill discipline was reported during the match between Swansea Town and Swansea Villa which ended 1-1, a most regrettable incident occurred at the termination of the game. One of the spectators rushed up to the referee Mr. Griff Rees, who had discharged his duties in that capacity in an impartial and able manner, and dealt him a severe blow in the face, whereupon Mr. Rees retaliated and a scene of general disorder followed, the referee subsequently leaving the ground under escort.

Although a representative town team was still five years away, the popularity of the game was growing fast - at the expense, it seems, of the sister code. There would be thirty two applications to join the Swansea & District League, which would make it twice the size of the local rugby league. Under the headline 'Will "soccer" come', the Leader essayed a glimpse into the future:

The impression that the Welsh (Rugby) Union have more to fear from the 'soccer' code than anything else is slowly but surely gaining ground.

It would not be a Town team who would take the initiative however, it would be the Swansea & District club East Side, who were responsible for bringing Bristol City Reserves of the Western League to the St. Thomas Athletic ground at the end of March. The game had been eagerly awaited since January, when the Leader, under the headline 'Crack Soccer Side to visit Swansea; Bristol City likely to come,' raised hopes of an appearance by their first team, Football League runners up the previous season:

> The development of soccer in Swansea has been pretty pronounced this season, and it is a sign of the times that a movement is now on foot to bring one of the crack English sides to the Town. The feeling is that if a side is selected from all the clubs affiliated to the Swansea & District Association League, they would be able to give even the best of talent a good game. And, besides, a visit from a crack English team would do much towards further stimulating interest in the soccer code. Just now the East Side club are busying themselves with a view to getting either Bristol City or Aston Villa to Swansea at the close of the present season. The chances of Bristol City consenting are said to be very favourable.

A Swansea & District League team was selected, but the team sent down on Thursday evening, 2nd April 1908, as the South Wales Daily News noted, was 'not of first class calibre.' The crowd of 1600, probably a record despite the drizzle, witnessed 'a splendid fight by the local men, although it was evident from the start that the visitors did not exert themselves to the full.' City won 3-2 after being 2-1 down at the interval, and the Swansea & District team was;

E. Fisher (East Side), J. Kieft (East Side), Arthur Savage (Swansea Town), H. Rowe (Mumbles Albion), I. Morgan (Port Talbot), Tom Arnold (East Side), J. Turvey (East Side), T. Williams (East

Side), Mark Glover (Swansea Town), A. Ford and J. Baxter (Mumbles Albion). The referee was Mr. D. J. Sambrook, who was much involved in the local Swansea League for many years.

Swansea Town retained the District League championship in this season 1907-08. Some fixtures had to be held over until the following season, Mond Nickel would finish runners up, followed by East Side, Mumbles Albion, Port Talbot, Neath, Morriston, Llanelly, Pontardawe, Manselton, Swansea Villa, St. Pauls, Ystalyfera, Briton Ferry and Onllwyn. All division winners received their medals from Dr. Carl Langer, Managing Director of the Mond Nickel Works, who also presented a Challenge Shield to the League. This Dr. Carl Langer Shield is still played for going into the new century.

The 1908-09 season saw the all conquering Swansea Town team finding it hard going in the Swansea & District League. With quite a few of their players leaving them for other local clubs they could only finish sixth, behind Morriston the champions, Port Talbot, Mond Nickel, Mumbles Albion and Neath. Below them come Swansea United reserves, Pontardawe, Llanelly, Briton Ferry and Swansea Villa. Swansea Villa lost all their games during this season, except for one draw, the club it seems would then fade into oblivion.

A Swansea & District League team took on the might of Bristol Rovers, then of the Southern League, at Danygraig on Thursday 29th April 1909. The Bristol Rovers side cruised to an 8-1 victory, with the local press regarding the match as a learning curve for the local League. 'Rambler' of the Leader completed his report saying, 'something learned is something gained, and those who were in the 'melee' and those who were around learned many a little trifle. But trifles make perfection, and this is the object in view'.

The 1909-10 season commenced with the Southern League endeavouring to win the South Wales area for the Association code. Swansea League records will show that Southern League officials urged local league clubs to play in friendly games against the likes of Aberdare, Ton Pentre and Merthyr, these valley teams having already joined the Southern League. Southern League officials also met with Messrs. Charles Jenkins, D. J. Sambrook and Aubrey Edwards of the Swansea & District League, and discussions took place as to the possibility of visits to the Town by the leading clubs of the Southern League to play local league sides. Negotiations bore fruit with the visit of Crystal Palace to Danygraig on Saturday 29th January 1910, efforts to secure St. Helens for the match having failed.

The Swansea & District league team for this important visit read as follows:
E. Fisher (Swansea United), A. Davies (Port Talbot), H. C. Pearman (Briton Ferry), Albert Smith (Morriston), Ivor Morgan (Captain, Port Talbot), Percy Jones (Swansea Town), Willie Messer (Belgrave), R. Coulson (Port Talbot), Mark Glover (Mumbles Albion), H. Payne (Llanelly) and T. Messer (Belgrave).
The Leader explained that:
Fisher, who belongs to St. Thomas, is recognised as one of the safest goalies in the principality. His selection was a foregone conclusion. So was that of Mark Glover. Last season he did great service for Mumbles Albion, and his fleetness of foot, coupled with his capacity to use his head and feet well, should be of great service on this occasion.

Palace 'who by no means took down their League XI, did not extend themselves to the utmost, 'but' provided a good exhibition of the dribbling code,' and won 3-2. Fisher and Willie Messer would go on to play for the Swans, but Percy Jones and Mark Glover would unfortunately be lost to local football.

At the start of the 1910/11 season, the Western Mail could look back on the remarkable growth of the 'Association Code' since the formation of the South Wales & Monmouthshire F. A. some seventeen years earlier. The number of clubs it reported, had increased from about two dozen to 262, progress being particularly pronounced since the 1905/06 season, when there was a fourfold increase. 'Soccerite' in the Western Mail had this explanation:

Association appeals to the spectators, who like to see the ball throughout the game. Modern rugby appears to endeavour to hide this necessary article as much as possible. With the advancement of Soccer has come the advancement of the clubs, until today the majority of them have enclosed grounds and are taking excellent 'gates' even in rugby strongholds. And with the increased financial status the code is bound to improve in all ways conducive to its becoming 'the' game of the nation.

Seventy five of the 262 clubs mentioned were members of the Swansea & District League, which could now boast of six divisions. The outstanding side of this season were undoubtedly Swansea United who had returned from the South Wales League to the Swansea League. They easily won the first division championship and were also the beaten finalists of the Challenge Cup. In this Challenge Cup final, the match with Morriston at the Mond Nickel works ground ended 0-0, the match attracting a reported crowd of between 4,000 and 5,000 (as compared with only 850 for the All Whites on the same day, April 29th 1911). The trophy which was then held over until September, Morriston being successful at the third attempt.

To illustrate how far the game had progressed in Swansea at that time was shown when, on the 27th April 1911 at Morriston, the Swansea & District League XI had only lost 1-0 to Cardiff City, then lying fourth in the second division of the Southern League. It was reported that the star of the Swansea League side was a Gwilym Gimblett of Morriston who was soon lost to local football when he signed for Bolton Wanderers.

The annual report of the Swansea League at the seasons end showed that seventy five clubs were now affiliated, whilst there were some 2,500 registered players.

Article from the Cambrian Leader September 4th, 1908.

Mr. T. R. Boyd, Chairman of Swansea United (formerly East Side) wrote denying that his Club had "poached" Mark Glover who last year played Swansea Town, as suggested by a correspondent. Glover has signed on for Swansea United and will also play as a professional.

Mr. Boyd said:- "There is not the slightest foundation in the statement re poaching by my Club. I challenge your correspondent or any other individual to prove a single case where we have during the three years I have been in office with the Club tried to entice a player from any other Club. We have not as yet stooped to any underhand methods in our efforts to raise a team or secure a ground, which is more than can be said for some clubs I know. I have no doubt that Mark Glover is quite prepared to speak for himself if need be. About the trouble that is likely to crop up when certain fixtures are played we are quite prepared for any trouble that may come".

With reference to that last paragraph, there are at least half a dozen clubs in the Swansea & District League who are determined not to play against sides which include professional players. Indeed there is prospect of the matter being brought up for discussion at the next League meeting. Swansea United have a perfect right to play any men they like, and to pay them what they like, and it seems a trifle inconsistent for the teams that are at present complaining, that they, without hesitation play against Ton Pentre and similar clubs who have half a dozen professionals. It would be a pity to see such an excellent combination as East Side deprived of fixtures, so it will be as well if the League come to some decision at once.

The statement has before been made that East Side have "poached" players, but the letter from Mr. Boyd ought to put a stop to any more such statements.

NOTE:- It was interesting to then note that Swansea United did start the season with a fixture against Morriston and drew the match 2-2, so hopefully the position was resolved to all clubs satisfaction.

It was around season 1907-08 that the Swansea League was fully established and the growth of this League increased so quickly that other senior divisions had to be instituted and by the season of 1910-11, six divisions had been formed.

The first known champions of the Senior Division of the League were Swansea Town, they won the inaugural official championship in season 1905-06 and then repeated the feat the following season, they would also win it in 1913-14 which was the last season before the first World War. The first Junior Section winners were Brunswick Mission, the League then decided that it would now form into divisions and by 1908-09 there were four such sections in being. Other winners in those very early days included such teams as Pentrechwyth, Belgrave, Llanelly, Plasmarl, Swansea United and Morriston, and in season 1912-13 the winners of the Senior Division were no less than Milford Town, this would emphasise the spread of teams in the Swansea League at the time.

The cup competitions didn't come into being until season 1908-09, with the successful clubs for these inaugural competitions being Mond Nickel Works in the Senior Cup, Llanelly in the Junior Cup, whilst the Dr. Carl Langer Shield was won by Morriston. This Mond Nickel side at the time would appear to have been a mighty force, not only did they win the first division championship in 1909-10 season but won the Senior Cup five times out of the first six competitions that were played before the first World War intervened. Interestingly enough, the last time the Mond Nickel Works name appears on the Swansea & District honours board was 1913-14, one would assume that after the resumption of fixtures after the war in 1919 that the club had moved on to another League.

During the years of the first World War 1914-18, all football in the area was abandoned, and it was not until season 1919-20 that saw the restart of local football. Naturally things took time to get underway and it was no surprise that the 1st and 5th Division Championships were not completed, but the season saw Gorseinon win the Senior Cup, Seven Sisters the Intermediate Cup and Morriston Villa the Junior Cup. Other division winners for this restart season saw Aberpergwm, Cwm Mission and Welsh Juniors among the honours.

The League continued to run six divisions and it is interesting to note that in seasons 1921-22 and 1922-23 the league also ran a Gower Division and a Neath Division. One would then suppose that with the advent of the West Wales F. A. being set up in 1922 then these divisions would have passed into their own area Leagues.

Due to the rapid advance of the Association code and the formation of other leagues in the areas of Neath, Llanelly and Pembrokeshire, it was decided by the South Wales and Monmouthshire F. A. Council that they would give self government to the Leagues administrators in the Western area. Thus the formation of the West Wales Football Association came into being in 1922. This Association would conduct the affairs of all local football from Briton Ferry to Pembrokeshire.

Mr. Charles Jenkins, one of the founders of the Swansea & District League, and its Secretary since its inception, left his position and took over as the first Secretary of the West Wales F. A.. It was a position that he would hold until Mr. S. B. Williams replaced him in 1946.

Meanwhile, his position as Secretary of the League was filled by Mr. W. H. Sparkes, who would hold the post until his sudden death in 1940.

The West Wales F. A. continues to this day to control the overall affairs of football in the area, the body has proved over the years to be an effective organisation and has always had a good working relationship with the Swansea League. Like the Swansea League, the West Wales has had many fine administrators over the years, in its seventy eight year history, there have only been seven Secretaries. The present incumbent, Mr. Bob Waygood, has been in the post for the past twenty two years and has always upheld the great tradition of his predecessors.

It was during season 1922-23 that saw the formation of the Hafod Brotherhood club, they would first play in the Swansea Sunday Schools League for one season, they then became members of the Swansea & District League the following year. Mention must be made of the fact that the Hafod Brotherhood club are the longest serving club in the history of the League, they have had unbroken service since joining the League in season 1923-24. It is a very proud record, and shows not only credit to the may fine players and officials over the years, but also the comradeship and loyalty that is sadly lacking as we go into a new century.

Whilst the Mond Nickel Works were the dominant force in the early years, even their successes were upstaged by the Cwm Athletic side of the twenties. Their record during this decade is one that has not been bettered up to the present day, in fact one would have to be very brave to suggest that their record will ever be surpassed.

Cwm Mission, A. F. C. 1921-22. "Joseph Janes" Cup Winners. Swansea & District Champions, 2nd Division.
Bowen, (Chairman). A. Morgan. T. Hardy. W. Blewett. R. Crocker. R. Cottel. W. Hellens. W. Davies.
J. Tomkins, (Treas). E. Porter. E. Charles. R. Smith. A. Bosser. P. John, (Trainer).
T. Teesdale. C. Thomas. T. Evans. B. Kelly, (Capt). W. McVeigh. F. Tomkins. J. Thomas, (Sec).
Jones. J. Teesdale. W. Phillips.

Swansea and District Association Football League. CWM ATHLETIC A. F. C. 1st Division Champions and Senior Cup Winners, 1922-3-4.
A. Roberts. (Comm.) D. Nelson. D. Nanteurvis.(Trainer) J. H. Tomkin. (Trainer) A. Bowen. (Chairman)
A. Blewett. (Comm.) I. Nichols, (Comm.) E. Martin. (Comm.) A. Rosser. Councillor Bart Cronin. E.Richards.
Mr. E. Edwards. (President) W. Davies. G. Teesdale. (Comm.) R. Voysey. (Secretary) D. Richards. T. Atherton.
R. Norman. E. Charles. B. Kelly. (Capt) T. Yates. W. McVeigh. F. E. Tomkins. J. Jones. W. Phillips.

During this period they won no fewer than five First Division championships, including four consecutive successes between 1923-24 and 1926-27, they also completed two hat tricks of consecutive Senior Cup triumphs in seven seasons, losing in the final of the one they missed out on. They would also in the twenties add to this impressive record by winning the West Wales Amateur Cup on four occasions and losing to Swansea Town in another final.

No one can ever dispute that at this time, the Cwm Athletic club were an incredible outfit, many older people often recall the exploits of this fine side when comparisons are being made. One would have to agree, that their record of success during this period, would make them candidates as one of the outstanding teams in the history of the League.

In spite of this success, it is interesting to note that, after their First Division championship win in season 1930-31, the Cwm Athletic club do not appear again on the Swansea League honours board until winning the Division 1 title again in season 1950-51. In the meantime however, they did win the West Wales Amateur cup again in 1949, beating Cwm Albion in the final. The Division 1 runners up award in 1951-52 was the last honour that this famous club achieved, as shortly after this they went out of existence.

No one side dominated the thirties, as in fact records show that the top division was won by a different side each season. It was a time though that quite a few clubs were beginning to emerge, clubs who would go on to be stalwart member clubs for many years to come. For instance, in season 1931-32, North End won their first ever honours as League members when they performed the First Division championship and Senior Cup double. These would be the first of many such honours that this illustrious club would achieve, and it would see them go on to become one of the most successful clubs in the history of the League.

The North End club only entered the League in season 1930-31, with records showing that their strip at that time was white shirts and black shorts. Their headquarters were at the Old Duke Hotel and they played their home matches at the New Park, Townhill.

North End quickly established themselves in the League. As stated earlier, they went on to win the Division One and Senior Cup double the following season with one unique and remarkable statistic arising from that Senior Cup win. The appearance of Willie McVeigh in the North End side meant that he had appeared in the last TEN consecutive Senior Cup finals. He had appeared in two finals for Cwm Mission, seven for Cwm Athletic and the tenth with North End, surely this record will never be equalled.

It was after this double winning season in 1931-32 that the club decided that they would move on to play in the Welsh League. Their application under the name of Swansea North End was successful and they were placed in the Welsh League Division Two Western section. Teams in this section would include the likes of Cornelly, Treorchy, Gwynfi, Llanelly and Swansea 'A'.

Unfortunately the venture was not a success and lack of funds meant that the club would pull out after one season. It was to be many years before the North End club were reformed and would be back in the Swansea League.

HAFOD BROTHERHOOD A. F. C.
Champions Division 3, Swansea Sunday Schools A. F. L., and Winners David Thomas Cup, Season 1926-27.

THE HIGHLY SUCCESSFUL HAFOD BROTHERHOOD SIDE OF 1937-38 SEASON.

Another successful side at this time were the Garthmoor club from the Neath district. They had a few championship and cup successes, as did Consolidated, Midland Athletic, Gordon Villa and Baldwins & Elba.

The League at this time were running five divisions, and this set up would continue up to the Second World War in 1939. Such was the strength of the League was shown by the fact that local teams were successful in seven out of the ten West Wales Amateur Cup competitions in the thirties. Alexandra were successful on three occasions whilst Hafod Brotherhood won it twice, other local successes were recorded by Skewen and Cwm Athletic.

The Hafod Brotherhood club were noted travellers in the pre-war years. Their fabled journeys started in 1930, when for four consecutive years the club visited London for Easter games. One of these trips was extended to take in a visit to Newhaven, where they took on and beat the local Town team who at the time were the champions of the Sussex League. It was during this period that the Hafod club felt the need to ease the difficulties of obtaining such fixtures and also saw the need to associate themselves with the Town on its travels. To this end, it was decided that the club would use the name 'Swansea Nomads' when playing matches outside the area. Further pre-war trips took in Paris in 1935, Brussels in 1936 and 1937, and Ilfracombe in 1938.

Mention must be made at this point in the League history, of the success of the Swansea Nomads in winning the South Wales & Monmouthshire Cup for the first time, with the club being the first Swansea Amateur side to win this coveted trophy. The Nomads team in their 3-1 victory over Porth was as follows:- Sam Ashton, Wilf Thomas, Bobby Williams, Glyn Whitter, Jack Lewis, Stan Richards, Trevor Jones, John Cooze, Haydn Tucker, Les Brown and Dick Penrose.

GWENT ATHLETIC A. F. C.

BRUNSWICK UNITED A. F. C. VETCH FIELD 1925-26.

Briton Ferry Athletic A. F. C. Swansea League Cup Final side at the Vetch Field, Swansea. Season 1930-31.
Back Row (Left to Right): H. Williams, G. Rees, T. Davies, J. Llewellyn, J. Evans, J. Reynolds, S. Lloyd, S. Parker.
Front Row (Left to Right): P. Reed, T. Thomas, V. Martin, R. Williams, M. Thomas.

GARDEN VILLAGE A. F. C. 1922-23 SEASON. First Season in Swansea & District League.

HAFOD BROTHERHOOD A. F. C. SEASON 1934-35.

ALEXANDRA A. F. C. 1936-37 WINNERS CARL LANGER SHIELD, SWANSEA & DISTRICT SENIOR CUP SWANS CHALLENGE CUP, ST. JOHN AMBULANCE CUP WEST WALES AMATEUR CUP.
Included: E. James, A. Mordan, G. Jones, J. James, Edwin Lewis, W. Pitson, Edward Lewis, I. Williams, J. Stokes, P. Pitson, H. Gibbons, H. Minney, J. Jones, C. Morris, T. Morgan, J. McCarthy, B. Jones, H. Davies, G. Panniers, J. Minty, C. J. Evans, E. Hill, Evan Rees, I. Richardson, S. Griffiths, I. Haste, F. Haines, J. Cooze, D. Cupid, G. Morgan, S. Spooner, A. Rees, E. Pope, G. Davies.

SWANSEA SENIOR LEAGUE COUNCIL MEETING 1937.

1930'S SWANSEA LEAGUE REPRESENTATIVE TEAM AT THE VETCH FIELD.
Fourth from right in back row is Mr. Bryn Williams League Secretary for many years.

KILVEY ATHLETIC
A Successful Season in the 1930's. Included in the group are the Captain Roy Williams and Secretary Arthur Peet.

CHAPTER 2 - THE FORTIES

On September 3rd 1939, the second world war was declared and all local Leagues in Swansea met and decided that they would suspend all activities agreeing that they would wait and see what transpired in the coming weeks. The English Football Association immediately cancelled all League matches and said that they would look into the possibility of setting up regional Leagues. This they would eventually do with Swansea Town playing in a Western Region containing clubs in the South Wales and South Western area of England.

At the 17th Annual General meeting of the West Wales Football association, held at the Y. M. C. A. on the 15th September 1939, the Secretary of the Association informed all those members present that all competitive football would be suspended but friendly matches would be permissible, he went on to say that these conditions may well be altered in the forthcoming weeks and informed members that so far 136 clubs had registered and that fourteen leagues and competitions had been sanctioned.

Even allowing for the fact that we were at war, there seemed to be a strong will to continue with local sport, Evening Post reports would show that other sports such as rugby, athletics, hockey and golf, were all eager to carry on providing for local sportsmen. On September 26th, the Swansea Sunday Schools League held a meeting and their Secretary, Mr. Ivor Davies, said that they would continue to provide football for Senior, under 20's and under 17 levels and urged clubs to contact him. This was followed by a meeting of the Swansea Thursday League on the 10th October and they again stated that they would also like to provide football for their members.

At a meeting of the Swansea Gwalia League at the Y. M. C. A. on October 11th, the Secretary, Mr. Bryn Williams, reported that their League, like the Swansea Senior League had received notification from the West Wales F. A. advising them of a lifting of the ban on local football and it was their opinion that as with immediate effect local league football should continue. It was also stated at this meeting that they were having great difficulty in obtaining the necessary number of teams to function, with this in mind it was suggested that the Swansea District League be contacted to highlight their problem of the shortage of players.

Arising from this request the following statement was issued on the 21st October 1939:-

Two of Swansea's biggest Amateur Soccer Leagues, the Swansea & District League and the Swansea Gwalia League are to be amalgamated, and their matches will be played as from November 7th under the auspices of the Swansea Gwalia Combination.

This important decision was reached at a meeting held at the Y. M. C. A. last evening, also attended by the Swansea Sunday Schools league, over which Mr. S. B. Williams (Swansea Town) presided, when it was resolved that "both the Swansea & District and Gwalia Leagues advise their clubs to join a new combination for the duration of the war years, jointly organised by the Leagues, to be known as the Swansea Gwalia Combination". The joint committee will meet next week to arrange fixtures for the clubs, then to commence on November 7th 1939.

Among those present at the conference of the Leagues were Messrs. Ivor Davies, D. O. Howell, C. Marles, A. R. Price, W. H. Sparkes, C. Harding, B. Williams, J. McIntyre and E. Williams. The elected officers of this new League were Chairman Mr. T. R. Evans, Secretary Mr. W. H. Sparkes, Treasurer Mr. Bryn Williams. Shortly after this conference, the elected Secretary, Mr. W. H. Sparkes passed away, it was agreed that he would be replaced by Mr. A. R. Price.

On Friday 6th November 1939, a General Meeting was held at the Y. M. C. A. when the decision of the both Leagues to combine was confirmed. The new combination would eventually consist of 23 clubs and the suggestions of Executive Committee and the Appeals Board were unanimously confirmed. The Chairman Mr. T. R. Evans, stated that the success of the combination rested with the clubs themselves, and he did not doubt that they would loyally carry out the fixtures and thus ensure a very successful season, notwithstanding the late start.

The following is the list of fixtures and referees for the first day of this historic combination for the war years, 7th November 1939.

Division 1

Baldwins	v	Bryn Juniors	E. J. Jones
Stepney	v	Montana	A. J. Guard
Mond Nickel	v	Plasmarl United	S. J. Norris
Cwm Albion	v	Hafod Brotherhood	A. E. Tucker
White Rose	v	National Oil Refinery	J. Griffiths
Gordon Villa	v	Prince of Wales Dry Dock	W. E. Rees

Division 2

Bryn Juniors	v	Baldwins	L. Burgess
M. C. A.	v	Players Welfare	J. W. Tribe
Upper Forest	v	Llansamlet Church	W. Court
Pen-y-Quar	v	Tegid United	S. J. Sterio

The step of the two Leagues working so well during the war years was so successful, that when hostilities ceased the members of the two league councils held a meeting at the Y. M. C. A. on the 13th May, 1946 and agreed to recommend to the clubs attached to the two leagues that they should amalgamate and form one strong league for the Swansea area. A meeting of the clubs was held at the Y. M. C. A. on June 17th 1946, sixty two clubs being in attendance and it was decided unanimously to accept the recommendation that the Swansea & District League and the Swansea Gwalia League should amalgamate, the league to become known as the Swansea District Gwalia League. The following officers were elected:-

Chairman	Mr. C. H. Marles.	**Vice-Chairman**	Mr. C. H. Harding.
Secretary	Mr. Bryn Williams.	**Treasurer**	Mr. R. O. Rees.
Asst. Secretary	Mr. A. R. Price.		

The handbook of the new Swansea District Gwalia Association league for 1946-47 shows that the league started with some fifty clubs, the roll call is as follows:-

Section 'A'	**Section 'B'**	**Section 'C'**
Bryn Athletic	East Dock Loco	Lady of Lourdes
Grovesend Welfare	N. O. R.	Consolidated Fisheries
Mond Nickel Works	Upper Forest Wel.	Penclawdd
Penllergaer	Bryn United	Dunvant
Cwm Albions	Clarence Untd.	Landore G. W. R.
Briton Ferry	Hafod Athletic	Rockspur
Rees & Kirby	Pontlliw Untd.	Loughor St. Michaels

Rockspur
Stepney
Celtic United
Hafod Brotherhood
C. Y. M. S.
Cwm Athletic
Mumbles
Glanrhyd Villa
L. M. S. Loco
Weavers Welfare
Danygraig Ath.
British Legion
Welsh Juniors
Baldwins
Mond Nickel
Winch Wen
Swansea Boys Club
Waunarllwydd
Tower United
P. O. Engineers
Port Tennant Corries.

Junior Division (under 19's)

Winch Wen
Baldwins Welfare
Llangyfelach
Elba Works 'A'
Celtic United
C. Y. M. S.
Elba Works 'B'
Albert Rovers

The first championship winners of this new league were Cwm Albions, Clarence and St. Michaels Loughor, whilst the cup winners were Grovesend, Clarence, Tower United and Llangyfelach. It was a very successful start to this new league and the following season of 1947-48 saw the membership rise to 84 clubs and then in 1948-49 season the League was running eight divisions to cater for the needs of local clubs.

At the end of the season 1947-48, the name of the League changed once again. At a meeting held at the Y. M. C. A. it was proposed and carried unanimously that the new name should be the Swansea Senior Association Football League, this name is still as it is today. It was at this time that local football was thriving, people were beginning to get over the horrors of the six war years, also the many local lads who had given valiant service for their country had now returned and were beginning to put the sad years behind them and return to their former clubs. We must also remember those who sadly did not return, and those who on returning never perhaps had the chance to play again.

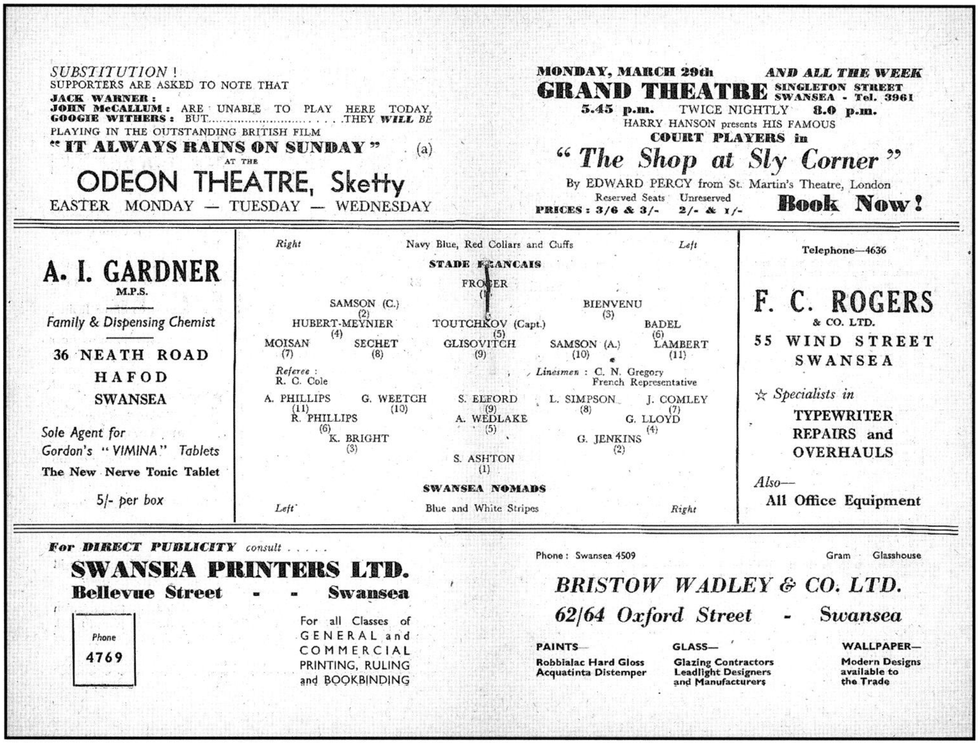
SUBSTITUTION !
SUPPORTERS ARE ASKED TO NOTE THAT
JACK WARNER :
JOHN McCALLUM : ARE UNABLE TO PLAY HERE TODAY,
GOOGIE WITHERS : BUT.............................THEY WILL BE
PLAYING IN THE OUTSTANDING BRITISH FILM
" IT ALWAYS RAINS ON SUNDAY " (a)
AT THE
ODEON THEATRE, Sketty
EASTER MONDAY — TUESDAY — WEDNESDAY

MONDAY, MARCH 29th AND ALL THE WEEK
GRAND THEATRE SINGLETON STREET SWANSEA - Tel. 3961
5.45 p.m. TWICE NIGHTLY 8.0 p.m.
HARRY HANSON presents HIS FAMOUS
COURT PLAYERS in
" The Shop at Sly Corner "
By EDWARD PERCY from St. Martin's Theatre, London
PRICES : Reserved Seats 3/6 & 3/- Unreserved 2/- & 1/- Book Now!

A. I. GARDNER
M.P.S.
Family & Dispensing Chemist
36 NEATH ROAD
HAFOD
SWANSEA
Sole Agent for
Gordon's "VIMINA" Tablets
The New Nerve Tonic Tablet
5/- per box

Navy Blue, Red Collars and Cuffs
STADE FRANCAIS
FROGER (1)
SAMSON (C.) (2)
BIENVENU (3)
HUBERT-MEYNIER (4)
TOUTCHKOV (Capt.) (5)
BADEL (6)
MOISAN (7)
SECHET (8)
GLISOVITCH (9)
SAMSON (A.) (10)
LAMBERT (11)

Referee : R. C. Cole
Linesmen : C. N. Gregory
French Representative

A. PHILLIPS (11)
G. WEETCH (10)
S. ELFORD (9)
L. SIMPSON (8)
J. COMLEY (7)
R. PHILLIPS (6)
A. WEDLAKE (5)
G. LLOYD (4)
K. BRIGHT (3)
G. JENKINS (2)
S. ASHTON (1)
SWANSEA NOMADS
Blue and White Stripes

Telephone—4636
F. C. ROGERS
& CO. LTD.
55 WIND STREET
SWANSEA
☆ Specialists in
TYPEWRITER
REPAIRS and
OVERHAULS
Also—
All Office Equipment

For DIRECT PUBLICITY consult .....
SWANSEA PRINTERS LTD.
Bellevue Street - - Swansea
Phone 4769
For all Classes of
GENERAL and
COMMERCIAL
PRINTING, RULING
and BOOKBINDING

Phone : Swansea 4509 Gram Glasshouse
BRISTOW WADLEY & CO. LTD.
62/64 Oxford Street - Swansea
PAINTS— Robbialac Hard Gloss, Acquatinta Distemper
GLASS— Glazing Contractors, Leadlight Designers and Manufacturers
WALLPAPER— Modern Designs available to the Trade

HAFOD BROTHERHOOD A. F. C. 1948-49.

To show the strength and feeling for local football at this time, on Easter Monday 1948, the Hafod Brotherhood club under their travelling name of Swansea Nomads, entertained the Stade Francais Club of Paris. The match at the Vetch Field attracted a crowd of over 8,000 spectators and saw the home side victorious by 5 goals to 4.

It is interesting to note from the Brotherhood Jubilee brochure that the visit of Stade Francais was a joint venture with perhaps one of the most famous of all Amateur Cup sides, the legendary Bishop Auckland. Each club paid a guarantee fee of £150 for a match in the North on the Saturday and at Swansea on the Easter Monday. The game with Bishop Auckland was drawn 4-4, this gives an indication of the strength of the then Nomads side to defeat such opposition. The Nomads team on that famous day:- Sam Ashton, Griff Jenkins and Ken Bright, Glyn Lloyd, Alan Wedlake, Dick Phillips, John Comley, Leon Simpson, Stan Elford, Gordon Weetch and Archie Phillips.

Before the start of the 1946-47 season the Swansea League received a letter from the Welsh F. A., the contents of which were unusual to say the least. They stated that all local leagues were banned from allowing the signing and playing of any German prisoners of war in their teams. It had come to their notice that certain clubs had made such signings.

There were quite a few German prisoners of war camps in Wales at the time, perhaps one of the biggest was on the outskirts of Bridgend, on the old A48 road. This is where the legendary Manchester City goalkeeper Bert Trautman spent some time, he would have been a useful signing for any local club. The Swansea League wrote to all its member clubs to comply with the Welsh F. A. request.

By the following season the League had expanded to six divisions and they were also requested to start an under nineteen section. As they had received applications from eleven clubs of this age group, the League duly started such a division.

One of the biggest headaches for the League at this time was the lack of pitches, and perhaps more importantly the standard of these venues to accommodate the leagues requirements. Urgent meetings were being held at the time with the then Parks Superintendent Mr. T. Winchcombe. He agreed that more facilities were urgently needed but stated that the Council were still recovering from the aftermath of the war and money for these facilities was in short supply.

Mr. Winchcombe also made it quite clear at the time, that at some venues, even though the pitches would be up to standard, the Council could not guarantee that they would be in a position to provide changing facilities. Such were the conditions at that time, that teams in our League were playing matches with no changing or washing facilities. It was a hard time and it has to be recorded that this state of affairs would continue until the early fifties.

We were at the time able to hold all our finals at the Vetch Field. There were always large crowds for these fixtures, minutes of the League show that the League Council members were at the time very upset because the Swansea Town Board had requested a ten per cent share of the gate proceeds. After much debate it was agreed that the League would accede to their request, even so, it left a bitter taste to some members. Records also show that because of the large crowds attending these finals, Council would also request and pay for the presence of two policemen, read into that what one wants.

The 1948 season saw the League once again expanding and the Secretary, Mr. Bryn Williams, informed Council that such was his workload, he felt it necessary to ask them to consider the purchase of both a typewriter and a duplicating machine. Some members at the time were very hesitant at such a request, records show that it took over twelve months for the Secretary to convince Council that this equipment was needed to keep pace with the everyday needs of running a League such as ours. Even then, when it was decided to obtain this needed equipment, Council went out and purchased a second hand typewriter and duplicator.

When one thinks back to these days and taking into account the number of teams in the League, one has to have great admiration for the way that the then officials and officers, carried out their duties and achieved such high standards. The typewriter situation brings to mind other such difficulties, hardly anyone in those days had motor cars, so to carry out everyday business meant a bus journey or perhaps more often than not one would have to walk. Even such a simple modern day thing as the telephone was only available to just a few people in the forties. It must have been a very difficult task being the secretary of a club in those days, but life progresses and one will perhaps look back and wonder how people coped at the time of the Millennium.

It was also agreed at the time that each retiring Chairman of the League, at the time up until 1954 it being on a yearly basis, would receive a suitable memento in appreciation of his year of office. It was agreed after much debate that the retiring Chairman would receive a memento, of his choice, but only up to the value of five guineas (£5.25). This gift to retiring Chairmen is still in being today, but the amount has kept pace with inflation.

Inter League games have always been an essential part of the League's history. After the war such fixtures were very popular with both players and officials alike. Council then decided that it would purchase its own kit for these matches, until now it had been the norm for the League to borrow a kit from one of its member clubs. There was however a major obstacle before the League could purchase a kit, as people would remember, at this time you had to be in possession of clothing coupons, a legacy of the war years, to buy any type of clothing. The League felt that the only way they could find the means of funding such a kit was to appeal to all its member clubs to donate coupons, then to ask the League's President and Vice-Presidents for the funds to purchase it. The League were grateful that the member clubs and League officials were more than happy to provide the necessary clothing coupons and money to achieve their aim.

An approach was then made to the then Town Clerk, Mr. T. B. Bowen, for permission for the League to use the Town's coat of arms motif on the jerseys, this request was refused. The kit was eventually purchased from Wilfred Harris sports shop, one of the few such outlets in the Town at that time.

The League broke new ground at the time by playing against the London Corinthian League, at the time one of the top teams in the London area. Thirteen players, accompanied by the League officers made the journey by train, leaving from High Street Station at 6.15 am on Saturday morning, returning the same evening. The match was lost by three goals to one, but it was noted that our share of the gate receipts came to £36.6.11d (£36.39p).

It was at the end of this 1948-49 season that the manager of the South Wales Builders, the biggest builders merchants in the Town at the time and one of the League's member clubs, presented a new trophy to the League, it would be called the Maes-Y-Gollen Cup.

The question of lack of pitches and facilities was growing in momentum. At the start of the 1949-50 season, representations were again made to the Town Council with regards to this lack of amenities. It got to the stage where one of our Vice Presidents, Mr. W. M. Leleu, stated that he would ensure that the local Evening Post would do everything it could to highlight the situation. He said that the newspaper would give the problem maximum coverage and would urge the local Council to provide more pitches and better facilities.

Mr. Winchcombe again appeared before League Council, once again stressing that whilst he

S. S. A. F. L. OFFICIALS AND PLAYERS AT HIGH STREET STATION EN ROUTE TO LONDON TO PLAY THE CORINTHIAN LEAGUE 1948.

1949 PRESENTATION OF THE MAES-Y-GOLLEN CUP TO THE LEAGUE.
MR. F. JONES, MANAGER OF SOUTH WALES BUILDERS LTD., HANDS OVER THE TROPHY TO MR. G. McINTYRE, THE LEAGUES CHAIRMAN.

sympathised with the League's position, he felt that everything possible was being done to alleviate the problems. He emphasised the fact that there were 113 teams playing in Swansea and that there were only 26 pitches. He went on to state that the huge upturn in interest in the Association code had brought with it the problem of finding enough pitches. League members once again urged the Swansea Council to find the means to not only provide more pitches, but also expressed the dire need of dressing rooms and washing facilities at existing pitches.

At further meetings with the local Council, members also put forward two areas which they thought were right for development, Clyne Valley racecourse, and the derelict site at Plasmarl. One would assume that the suggested Plasmarl site would be where the existing Morfa pitches are situated.

To attempt to obtain such funds, a National Jubilee Fund, also known as the Playing Fields Silver Campaign was set up. The proceeds of this National Fund would help with the provision of sporting facilities, collection boxes were passed around grounds on certain dates in Public Parks. The actual amount collected in the Swansea area was announced as £8.3.8d (£8.19p).

In 1949 the League appointed Mr. Abe Freedman, a prominent local businessman and Chairman of the Swansea Town Football club, as its President. It was a position he would fill for many years, giving outstanding service to both the League, and to local football. In his initial address to Council, Mr. Freedman expressed the need for anyone who saw an outstanding talent on the local parks, to contact Messrs. McCandless, Sykes or Barson at the Vetch Field. He went on to say that the Vetch Field and the Club would provide the necessary tuition to follow, as it was his belief that no local talent should slip the net. At his first meeting, he also provided a new trophy for the League, which would subsequently be named the Swansea Junior Cup.

The honours board for the post war years showed a bit of a mixed bunch, no one side would dominate these years. Cwm Athletic were again a force to be reckoned with, even though they had no honours to show for this period. It would be season 1950-51 before they would again win the Division 1 championship. Stepney were another side who were particularly strong a this time, they were Division 1 runners up in 1948-49, and they went one better by winning the championship the following season. They were also the Senior Cup winners in season 1948-49. The first four seasons after the war saw four different clubs win the Division 1 championship, the successful clubs being Cwm Albions, Briton Ferry, Midland Athletic and Stepney. It is pleasing to record that, apart from a spell out of the League some years later, Cwm Albions are still members of the Senior League.

In the cup competitions, again the honours were spread, Grovesend Welfare, Hafod Brotherhood, Stepney and Ivorites United were the successful clubs in this period. Again it was a barren spell for the formidable Cwm Athletic side, they appeared in two successive finals only to be beaten in both.

The passing of the 1940's would not be complete without relating to two players, Trevor Ford and Jack Kelsey, both of whom played in the Senior League in this era and went on to become two of perhaps Wales' finest footballers. If either of these players were playing in today's football, they would be classed as superstars and be afforded the glory and adulation that today's so called stars get.

Trevor Ford left school at fourteen and found employment in the local steelworks, he then signed and played two seasons with Tower United, playing at the time as a full back. In his own words he was slim and a bit weak, he needed to toughen up to survive in such company.

After being spotted playing for Tower by the then Arsenal Chief Scout, Arthur Lindon, he was offered amateur terms by the club, these he turned down as he was set on signing for the Swans. He

THE FIRST STEPS TO GLORY - SKIPPERING THE SCHOOL SIDE AT POWYS AVENUE.

TREVOR IN ACTION FOR SUNDERLAND.

eventually signed professional forms for the Swans in 1943, he then went on to complete his National Service where he first appeared as a centre forward. In his first full season in full time soccer, he scored 41 goals in a revamped Football League Southern section in season 1945-46.

He went on to play for Aston Villa, Sunderland, Cardiff City, PSV Eindhoven and Newport County, he also represented Wales on 38 occasions.

Jack Kelsey also left school at fourteen and found employment at the Swansea Vale works, he played his football for both the junior and senior sides with the Winch Wen club. It was during a vital league match against the Ivorites in 1949 that Jack, after having a blinder and saving two penalties, both incidentally taken by the then Arsenal Scout and Ivorites stalwart Les Morris, was first noticed.

It was Les Morris' persuasion that finally took Jack to Arsenal, he was a model one club professional, breaking into the first team in 1953 and giving the Arsenal club and Wales magnificent service over many years. He was in 1955, selected for the Great Britain team against the Rest of the World, played in the 1958 World Cup finals in Sweden, and altogether won 41 caps for Wales.

It had been an eventful few years since the second world war, the amalgamation of the local leagues had been an outstanding success. The Secretary, Mr. Bryn Williams, said that the League would go on from strength to strength, he was thrilled by the huge upsurge in local football. He went on to say that the Swansea Senior League would continue to provide the platform for competition in the area.

JACK KELSEY SAVING AT THE FEET OF SPURS' DAVE DUNMORE IN A LEAGUE MATCH AT HIGHBURY STADIUM, 1953.

SOUTH WALES BUILDERS XI 1949-50.

CWM ATHLETIC 1949-50.

MIDLAND ATHLETIC S. S. A. F. L. DIVISION ONE CHAMPIONS 1948-1949.

ST. PAUL'S A. F. C.
WINNERS - SWANS NURSERY CUP 1948-49.

CWMFELIN PRESS A. F. C. 1947-48.
BACK: H. KELLY, T. THOMAS, J. REED, K. THOMAS, H. RICHARDS, A. RIDGWAY, I. SLATTERY, A. BOLAND, (WORKS MANAGER), I. DAVIES, E. SCREEN, C. WEATHERLY, D. PARNELL.
FRONT: G. OWEN, T. LYNCH, W. FROVINE, P. CARTER, G. WILKINS. RIDGWAY (MASCOT).

GWENT A. F. C.

MR. T. R. EVANS ONE OF THE FOUNDER MEMBERS OF THE SWANSEA SENIOR LEAGUE BEING WELCOMED BY MR. ABE FREEDMAN.
L. TO R.: MR. J. THOMAS, MR. E. G. WILLIAMS, MR. T. R. EVANS, MR. A. BEAL, MR. FREEDMAN (PRESIDENT) AND MR. B. WILLIAMS (SECRETARY).

PORT TENNANT STARS A. F. C. 1947-48
THE FIRST EVER STARS SIDE INCLUDING THE PRESIDENT MRS. DAVEY, CHAIRMAN T. ASQUITH AND LONG SERVING MEMBERS MESSRS. A. MAINWARING AND T. RONAN.

CHAPTER 3 - THE FIFTIES

The start of the 1950-51 season was hit by a Council workers strike, which meant that the first three weeks of the season would be lost. In those days the League didn't operate an evening series of fixtures, this was due to the long hours of work and for players in those days perhaps having to make two bus journeys to get to a match. That of course was if they could afford the bus fares.

Evening games were only played at the seasons end, and this would only be if it was absolutely imperative to do so. This meant that it was very difficult for the Secretary to complete the seasons fixtures. The last thing he would want is a delayed start to the season when the weather is at its best.

It is hard to believe that it was 1950 before the Secretary asked the League Council to allow him to have a telephone installed. It was such a big decision at the time that it was nearly another year before he would have a telephone connected to his home. One can only marvel at the way the Secretary at those times carried out the League programme. Even with the installation of a telephone, one would doubt whether he would be able to contact clubs as very few people had phones at the time.

Just as it is today, the shortage of referees was causing the League huge problems, repeated requests for new recruits fell on deaf ears. It is a problem which over the years has never been overcome, only further emphasising the importance of the referee to any League.

An interesting debate arose at the time when the West Wales F. A. suspended a referee because he was over fifty, thank goodness this ruling hasn't applied for some years now as quite a few of our referees have officiated well after their 50th birthday. Many players will remember such referees as Len Williams, Ned Edwards, Reg John, Arthur Davies and Vince Frendo, they were all referees who gave service well after this age. They were also great characters and referees who were well respected. On a lighter note, one would remember that Frank Sullivan retired three or four times after this age.

Another shortage at the time was the provision of goal nets, this was another problem that today's players wouldn't appreciate, but to play with nets in the fifties was a rarity, and as players of the day will recall, would at times cause massive arguments at matches. Representations were made to the Parks Department, their reply was that whilst they realised it was a problem it wasn't part of the permit payment. They added that they could not afford to supply them and that they had no immediate intentions of purchasing them. They did concede though, that if any club supplied their own nets, then the Council would provide suitable storage space for them at the grounds on which they played.

At the end of the 1950-51 season, the West Wales F. A. were attempting to introduce a new resolution which at the time left the Secretary, League representatives of the W. W. F. A. and all League Council wondering what games they were attempting to play. This resolution was such worded that "No League or competition shall include more than 50 clubs without the prior sanction of the West Wales F. A.." Everyone connected with local football pondered what the W. W. F. A. were trying to achieve, the Swansea Senior League had been in existence since 1901 and was providing football for over 100 clubs. The West Wales F. A. didn't come into existence until 1922, so one seriously had to wonder what they really had in mind. Perhaps it was just a case of them flexing their muscles. The Swansea League informed the W. W. F. A. that they would respond to their resolution at the next Annual Meeting, they informed them that Mr. I. V. Jones, Life Member and a member of the Welsh F. A., would represent them at this meeting. The West Wales F. A. must have had a rethink as the resolution was not presented at the Annual Meeting and has not been presented ever since.

Further concern was expressed to Swansea City Council at the start of the 1951 season, as to the condition of pitches and playing facilities. Such pressure was applied that both the Parks Superintendent, Mr. T. Winchcombe, and the Mayor at the time, both felt fit to appear before a full meeting of Council. The Mayor spoke at length and once again portrayed the same story, money was tight and they were doing all that they could to update facilities. He went on to say that our biggest problem was that there were too many teams for the amount of pitches available. He complimented the League on its work for the young men of the Town, he felt that organised football was an essential outlet for young people and hoped that the League would continue to thrive. He promised to ensure that the Swansea Council would do everything in its power to improve facilities.

It was at this time that the League first made contact with the Birmingham Works League, it was to be the start of many inter league matches between the two associations over the next twenty five years. The Birmingham Works League, like ourselves, were one of the biggest Leagues in the country at the time, they even had a full time Secretary and he was based at the League's office which was in the City centre.

Inter-league matches were to become a regular event, played annually, each association taking it in turns to play host and they were matches which were looked forward to with great anticipation. Many players of yesteryear will recall the honour to be called up for one of these games, it was almost like winning a cap. Those were the days when representing the League was looked on as an honour, sadly those days are gone. In the eighties, many is the time when the League found it difficult to field a full strength squad, due in the main to players just not making the effort.

The first fixture against the Birmingham League took place in 1950, such was the success of this encounter that it was decided to ask the Works League to play against the Swansea League in their 50 year celebration match.

The following report appeared in the South Wales Evening Post
Football for the season 1950-1951:

SWANSEA SENIOR FOOTBALL LEAGUE WILL HAVE MORE CLUBS

Ninety eight clubs participated in what was the best post war season for the Swansea Senior League, writes Bill Paton. Generally the standard was higher, and there was a keen struggle for honours in most of the divisions.

Two teams - Electric Welfare and Rockspur - were responsible for outstanding performances, completing the programme without losing a game. Both clubs only dropped two points.

In Division 8, St. Paul's and the Building Apprentices tied on points, and in a subsequent play-off St. Paul's won by three goals to two after extra time, thus retaining the championship for the second consecutive season.

In the First Division, Stepney, pipped on the post last year, won the honours after a keen struggle with Ivorites, who had some consolation by winning the Senior Cup. The Swans Nursery Cup - up for competition for the first time - went to Cwm Albions, one of the oldest clubs in the town.

In fact, the Cup competitions created more interest than ever. The Ivorites-Cwm Athletic clash was a real thriller, with the Fforestfach team getting the honours after a replay.

Prospects for the coming season are particularly rosy. Energetic secretary Mr. Bryn Williams tells us that there will be at least a dozen or more clubs. The only fly in the ointment is the shortage of playing pitches, but the League is paying close attention to this difficult problem and are hoping the coming season will bring an improvement to the position.

Final positions in each division and cup winners were:

Division 1	Stepney	Senior Cup	Ivorites
Division 2	East Side B. R.	Gwalia Cup	Samlet Stars
Division 3	Nelson	Intermediate Cup	Grovesend
Division 4	Electric Welfare	Nursery Cup	Cwm Albions
Division 5	Gorseinon B. L.	Maes-Y-Gollen Cup	Rockspur
Division 6	Treboeth		
Division 7	Rockspur		
Division 8	St. Pauls		

JUBILEE SEASON 1951-1952.

The Officers of the League for this season were as follows:-

President:	Mr. Abe Freedman.
Chairman:	Mr. Tom Day.
Vice-Chairman:	Mr. J. M. Rees (subsequently retired and replaced by Mr. F. Gabriel).
Hon. Secretary:	Mr. Bryn Williams.
Hon. Treasurer:	Mr. E. G. Williams.
Asst. Secretary:	Mr. A. R. Price.

Reading from the Minute Book of the League Council for the 1951-52 season the celebration of the 50 year Jubilee season seemed to start off on a low key. One would suppose that with the second world war not that long over and people recovering from the aftermath of this terrible period, priorities would be different in those days. It wasn't until a full Council Meeting on the 8th October 1951, that mention is first made of the Jubilee Year. Mr. Day the Chairman, appealed for all clubs to co-operate to make the Jubilee season a successful one. Mr. Williams the Secretary, stated that various suggestions would be put forward to the clubs during the season to mark the Jubilee, such as a return fixture with the Birmingham Works League and a League Dinner and Dance, he urged all clubs to give their full support to these ventures.

It was eventually decided by Council that arrangements would be made to celebrate the Jubilee season by playing a fixture against the Birmingham Works League and afterwards holding a celebration Dinner in the evening. It was also resolved that the Jubilee function would be called the League Celebration Dinner. Mr. Lee, Secretary of the Birmingham Works League, had written to confirm that his Association were honoured to be asked and were pleased to accept the invitation. It was also confirmed that Swansea Town A. F. C. had agreed to use of the Vetch Field for the game and that the date would be Tuesday, 15th April 1952.

With the confirmation of the date and venue, arrangements then had to be made for the after match celebration Dinner. When enquiries were returned, it was decided to accept the quotation received from the Mackworth Hotel in High Street. Their quotation was for Lunch to be provided at 7s 6d (38pence) and the evening Dinner at 9s 0d (45 pence) per head, the League also decided that they would make the

Mackworth Hotel their headquarters for the day's celebrations. It was also confirmed that the Birmingham party, numbering thirty six people, would be arriving by train at High Street Station at 12 noon and would be met and accompanied by League officials to the luncheon at the Hotel.

For the Luncheon it was resolved that invitations would be extended to His Worship the Mayor Alderman Dan Jones J. P., the League President Mr. Abe Freedman, and the full Council of the League bringing the total to sixty one guests. For the evening Celebration Dinner the party would consist of players and officials of both the Birmingham and Swansea teams, twenty two members of Council, ten Vice-Presidents, His Worship the Mayor, the League President, the Secretary of the Welsh F. A. Mr. Herbert Powell, the Secretary of the South Wales and Monmouthshire F. A. Mr. Russell, the Chairman of the Referees Society and Mr. Grove the Auditor, this making the total of ninety four guests.

Forms were also sent to all League clubs asking them to participate in the evening function at a cost of 10s 6d (53 pence) per ticket. It was also decided that the evening's entertainment would be provided by the Bonymaen Community Centre Male Voice Choir for which a donation of £2 2s 0d (£2.10p) would be paid. It was also agreed that programmes would be printed and sold prior to the match and admittance charges were set at Grandstand 1s 6d (8 pence) and to the field 1s 0d (5 pence). It was a most successful day, a large crowd at the Vetch Field saw the Birmingham League beat the Swansea League by 2 goals to nil. At the evening's reception Mr. Powell thanked all officers for their hard work in organising such a day and wished the Swansea Senior Football League every success for the next 50 years. Mr. Freedman responded on behalf of the Swansea League and thanked all the visitors and guests and also the Birmingham Works League, for travelling and taking part in the match and wished them every success for the future.

S. S. A. F. L. 50 YEAR CELEBRATION MATCH V BIRMINGHAM WORKS LEAGUE APRIL 1952. PICTURE AT MACKWORTH HOTEL SHOWS OFFICIALS OF BOTH LEAGUES PLUS GUESTS AND THE MAYOR ALD. DAN JONES.

1902 1952

Jubilee Celebration Dinner

at the

Mackworth Hotel, Swansea.

on

TUESDAY, APRIL 15th. 1952

Guests :

The Birmingham Works Amateur Football Association Council, Officials & Players.

1902 1952

Souvenir Programme

Inter - League Match

****

ON TUESDAY, 15th APRIL 1952

Birmingham Works Amateur Football Association

V

Swansea Senior Association Football League

at the

Vetch Field, Swansea

Kick - off 3 - 15 p. m.

****

His Worship The Mayor of Swansea Ald. Daniel Jones J. P. will kick off

SWANSEA SENIOR LEAGUE XI V BIRMINGHAM WORKS LEAGUE GOLDEN JUBILEE MATCH AT VETCH FIELD APRIL 1952.

SWANSEA SENIOR LEAGUE JUNIOR XI PLAYED AGAINST BIRMINGHAM LEAGUE 1951-52.

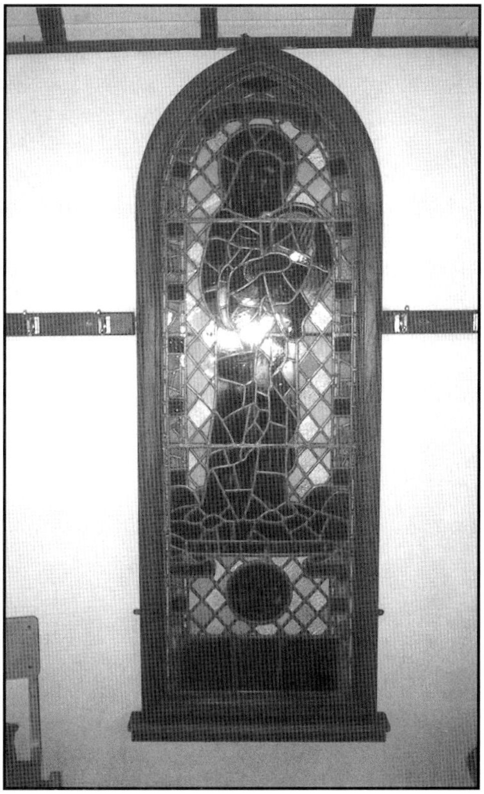

THE MEMORIAL PLAQUE AND WINDOW AT SKETTY BAPTIST CHURCH IN MEMORY OF MR. CHARLES JENKINS.

In 1953 the League lost one of its most senior members with the death of Mr. Charles Jenkins. Mr. Jenkins was one of the original founders of the Swansea League in 1901. One could say that he was the father of the League, not only did he help to set up the League but he was also the first Secretary and held the position until 1922. He then took over as Secretary of the newly formed West Wales F. A. in 1922 and he was to hold the position up until the second world war in 1939. In football terms the man was a giant and can rightfully take credit for the creation of perhaps one of the biggest and best Leagues in the country. Mr. Jenkins' memory was to be honoured at a memorial service on November 18th 1953, where at Sketty Baptist Church a plaque was unveiled paying tribute to all that he had achieved for local sport.

One thing the League couldn't be accused of at these times was waste, the second hand typewriter the League obtained at the end of the forties was now becoming obsolete, Council allowed the Secretary to purchase a new one for £29 but he was also told that he would have to sell the old one as part of the deal, Council accepted the offer of £2 from the Asst. Secretary Mr. A. Price. Earlier mention had been made of Jack Kelsey, it was in 1954 that Jack was awarded his first cap against Northern Ireland, the League sent a congratulatory telegram and all local sportsmen were delighted with the news.

Such was the attraction of the annual fixture with the Birmingham Works League that for the game in 1954, incidentally played at the Vetch Field, Council decided that it would cancel all its League games for that Saturday. The Birmingham team were entertained for lunch and evening dinner at the Embassy Club in the town centre, the guest speakers being Mr. Abe Freedman the League President and Mr. E. Taylor, the Chairman of the West Wales F. A.. The Senior League team on this occasion was J. Nevis (Danygraig), I. Campbell (Hafod Bro.), D. Robinson (Gors), G. Nurse (Penclawdd), A. Wedlake (Hafod Bro.), B. Hoppe (Mumbles Albion), J. Jackson (St. Augustines), I. Williams (R. T. B. Landore), B. Coates (Swansea B. C.), P. Grills (Swansea B. C.), and L Beynon (South Gower). The reserves were H. Britton (Stepney), S Harding (Cwm Albion), and T. Cullen (North End). Mr. Jack Thomas was the Team Manager. An excellent match saw the Swansea League claim victory by 3 goals to 2, the match once again highlighting the potential of these two fine sides. The Birmingham Works League repaid the Swansea League the compliment of inviting them to celebrate their Jubilee Season, invitations to their celebration dinner saw the Secretary Bryn Williams and the Chairman Mr. T. J. Richards attend the dinner in Birmingham.

1955 was a year when the weather badly affected the Leagues fixtures, there were great fears that we would not be able to complete our competitions. The Welsh F. A. were approached as to whether we could extend the season and in certain cases, matches in the W. W. F. A. Cup and League cups affecting teams in our League would also count as League fixtures as well. The request to the Welsh F. A. was granted and enabled the League to complete its programme.

In November 1955, there was strong talk regarding the formation of a Thursday League, records would show that there was such a league in existence for a time before the second world war. The purpose of such a league was originally to cater for players who worked at weekends, they traditionally then had early closing at their businesses or stores on Thursdays. Representations were made to the Senior League as to them formulating such a venture. Council's thoughts were that if such a league were to start, then it should come under the umbrella of the Senior League.

At a special meeting on January 18th 1956, the representatives of the Thursday League informed Council that they would prefer to set up their own administration, they also said that they would need the help of the Senior League to set up such a venture. A Thursday League would eventually become a reality, but it would be some years later.

It was also at this time that the League received correspondence from the Welsh F. A. with regards to a new innovation, the use of aluminium studs. These new studs had just been released on the market and the governing body felt the need to give guidance to eliminate injuries from any misuse by players.

It was also the year that the League received many complaints as to the condition and injuries thus caused by the playing surface at Hafod Park. They decided that they would inform clubs that if they wished not to play at this venue, then they would receive full backing of the League. Eventually the League informed the Parks Department that they would not be taking out any more permits at Hafod Park, obviously this would mean losing another venue.

Concern was also being expressed at this time as to teams playing on such venues as Graig Park, and also at the ash pitch at Paradise Park. As regards to these two venues, the League informed clubs that if they insisted on playing on these pitches, then any disputes that arose would be the clubs responsibility.

For the 1956 inter league match at R. T. B. Landore, it was unanimously agreed by Council that in future they would not select any player who had signed and played in the Welsh League. This ruling had been the subject of Council debate for many years, until now the barring of these players had always been defeated.

The League at the time were in the habit of holding trial matches before selecting their representative sides. It was at such a trial at Cwmbwrla Park in 1956, that such an outstanding display by one of its young players, saw him immediately selected for the League team at the after match selection meeting. The young player was Brian Purcell of Waun Wen, little did anyone know at the time that the Swans were in attendance at this trial. Brian was offered terms at the Vetch and had signed within days, his place in the League team going to Ivor Robinson of the Gors.

Brian went on to become a regular first team player at the Vetch Field for many years. It was such a tragic loss when Brian, and another local lad who had also given such great service to the Swansea club, Roy Evans, were killed in a car crash on the Heads of the Valley road whilst on their way to a match.

Early in the 1950's, the League had lost one of its founder members with the death of Mr. Charles Jenkins. Then in 1958-59, the League were to lose another two of its stalwart members within months of each other, when Mr. T. R. Evans and Mr. David Jones, both partner members in the formation of the League with Mr. Jenkins, passed away. It was sad, that in the space of just a few years, the League should lose its three founder members. These three founder members were giants in the game at local level, the League owes each gentlemen a great debt. At roughly the same time, another league stalwart, Mr. Tom Cole, passed away, here again was a man who had given so much to local football.

It was at this time that the League and its clubs were asked if they would contribute to the St. Mary's Church Appeal. The church had been extensively damaged by German bombers in the second world war and it was now to be reconsecrated on May 28th 1959. Between the contributions of both the League and its clubs, enough money was raised to purchase a chancery stool for the altar at the church and on the stool is the inscription 'To the Glory of God - The gift of the Swansea Senior Football League'.

One of the outstanding achievements of the 1950's was the feat of Swansea Boys Club in winning the Senior Cup in three consecutive seasons, which was only the fourth time in the history of the League that this feat had been achieved. Mond Nickel Works had achieved it in seasons 1912-13-14, and Cwm

THE CHANCERY STOOL PRESENTED TO ST. MARY'S CHURCH BY THE SENIOR LEAGUE AT ITS RECONSECRATION MAY 1959.

THE ALL CONQUERING 1950'S SWANSEA BOYS CLUB.
BACK (L. TO R.): J. McINTEE, C. JONES, D. PHILLIPS, B. REES, B. McCARTHY. FRONT (L. TO R.): R. GWYNNE, J. LAURIE, K. LOCKETT, P. GRILLS, B. COATES, B. LEE.

Athletic in 1925-26-27. Cwm Athletic then once again produced the treble by winning it in 1929-30-31 seasons.

The rarity of this achievement showed the strength of the fifties Boys Club side. On top of this they were also the Division 1 runners up on three occasions. One of their biggest rivals in this decade were the Port Tennant Stars side, not only would one say that they were one of the top teams, but surely one of the unluckiest. They were Senior Cup runners up on no fewer than five occasions, add to this the fact that they were also Division 1 runners up three times, it was no wonder that people called them the proverbial bridesmaids.

In the League's top division, the honours were evenly spread, no one side winning it on more than one occasion. That is until the last two seasons of the fifties when North End embarked on an unbelievable run of success. They won the Division 1 championship in 1958-59 and the 1959-60 seasons and would go on to complete the treble by winning it again in 1960-61 season. This was only the second time that any club had won three consecutive Division 1 championships. The first were the great Cwm Athletic side of the twenties, who in fact won the championship in four consecutive years, in seasons 1924-25-26-27. It was a wonderful achievement by a very good North End side and was to be the springboard to the enormous success that they have achieved over the years.

Another side that was starting to make a name for themselves at the end of the fifties was the works side Unit Colts. They started off in the Junior League in 1955, they then entered the Senior League and in 1959-60 season, carried off the Division 4 championship. It was to be the first of many successes over the next fifteen years.

The fifties had seen the League make rapid progress, whilst the late forties saw the local clubs re-establishing themselves after the war years, the League was now flourishing and with it saw the formation of some very strong sides. One very interesting point with regards to the West Wales Intermediate Cup, as in the 1940's no Swansea League side would win the trophy. Plasmarl United, Gors and Dillwyn Amateurs all reached the final but were all unsuccessful.

It had been a barren time for our clubs in this competition since the war, it was not until 1968 that a Swansea League side would eventually win the trophy, Ragged School becoming the first to do so.

Further reading of the history of the League will clearly show that this trend has been well and truly laid, more of that later.

SWANSEA DOCKERS - 1950.
BACK L. TO R.: W. CORNELL, T. HAMMETT, E. SCOTT, D. WILLIAMS, E. GAMMON, J. QUINN, H. DAVIES.
FRONT: R. KENNEDY, B. BEER, T. HILTON, W. PARKIN, M. THOMAS.

PORT TENNANT STARS 1950-51.
BACK: T. DOLPHIN, G. PHILLIPS, G. KEEPERS, R. SMITH, T. BECKERS, I. EDWARDS, E. CLEMENT, P. DORRELL. FRONT: R. BEAUJEAN, J. FERMANDELL, G. HURLOW, R. LEY, H. DAVIES.

*ATLAS SPORTS V BETTWS. VETCH FIELD 1952. WEST WALES F. A. AMATEUR CUP FINAL.
BACK L. TO R.: EDDIE DAVIES, LEN HILL, ERNIE ROBINS, CYRIL JOHN, RAY EVANS, NORMAN THOMAS.
FRONT: ERNIE OWEN, ISLWYN JONES, H. PHIPPS (CHAIRMAN), GWYN WILLIAMS, TOMMY LEWIS, GWYN LLOYD.*

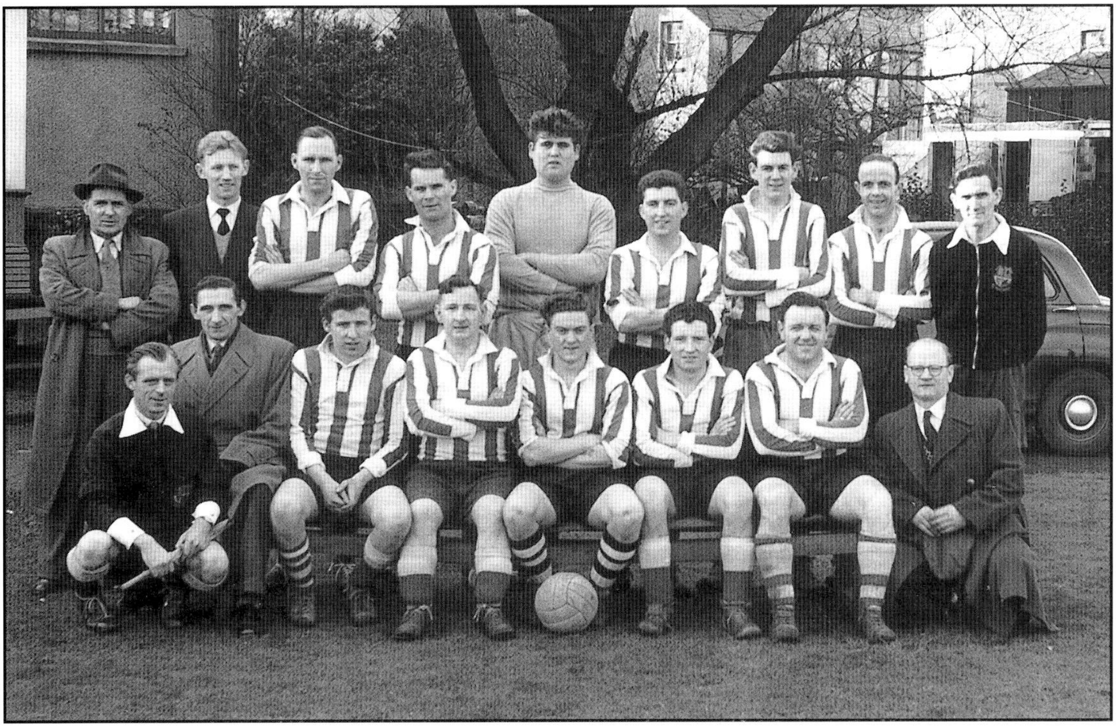

CWMFELIN PRESS A. F. C. GROUP INCLUDES D. JONES, G. HARRIS, C. JONES, G. BIDDER, B. BEYNON, H. MATHEWS, D. KERVIN, H. CRAVEN, J. COMLEY.

TOWER UNITED ON TOUR LONDON 1951.
THIRD FROM RIGHT IN BACK ROW IS ARTHUR HARRIS WHILST ON THE EXTREME LEFT IS HIS FATHER.

SWANSEA SENIOR LEAGUE V PEMBROKE.
BACK L. TO R.: J. LAURIE, R. THOMAS, J. NEVIS, W. JAMES, B. CASEY, T. MILLS. FRONT: B. O'REILLY, I. ROBINSON, G. RILEY, D. LAMBOURNE, C. JONES.

FFORESTFACH A. F. C. PRESENTATION DINNER 1952.
BACK: MR. & MRS. A. JONES, MR. & MRS. F. DAVIES, MR. OSSIE REES, MR. H. PECK, MR. G. HUGHES, MR. R. WILLIAMS, MR. L. WITHERS, MR. BRYN WILLIAMS, MR. & MRS. E. WILLIAMS. FRONT: MR. & MRS. E. PHIPPS, MR. & MRS. L. THOMAS, MR. & MRS. D. MORRIS, MR. P. McGILLVARY.

WAUN WEN A. F. C.
BACK L. TO R.: R. ABSOLAM, H. NORMAN, D. JAMES, P. NORMAN, G. JONES, J. WILLIAMS, T. ABSOLAM, G. JONES, L. DAVIES. FRONT: B. NORMAN, W. NORMAN, D. DRAPER, E. WILLIAMS, J. LEWIS, R. WILLIAMS.

SWANSEA SENIOR LEAGUE XI V BIRMINGHAM WORKS A. F. C.
AT WOLSELEY ATHLETIC GROUND, BIRMINGHAM, SATURDAY NOVEMBER 28TH 1953.

NORTH END A. F. C. 1958
BACK: J. SMITH (TRAINER), K. CHARD, J. DOLLARD, R. THOMAS, G. DAVIES, T. THOMAS, C. BARRY.
FRONT: H. DAVIES, R. POPHAM, G. NEWCOMBE, D. JENKINS, J. HOLE.

SWANSEA SENIOR LEAGUE XI 1958-59.
BACK L-R: R. THOMAS, G. DAVIES, A. MARSHALL, B. HOPPE, C. CHISLETT, P. LUCAS, J. THOMAS (MANAGER). FRONT L-R: G. EVANS, B. SWEENEY, D. LEWIS, G. NEWCOMBE, D. LAMBOURNE.

BACK ROW: T. HARRIS, J. CARROL, L. WALSH, MOORE? J. JONES, R. HART, E. SCREEN, D. DAVIES, K. EVANS, D. MARTIN, L. PENNOCK? F. LONG, C. HUGHES, D. WALSH? SECOND ROW: C. DAVIES, L. DAVIES, R. MADDOCKS, J. HART (CART), G. JONES, R. SCREEN, HUMPHREY. BOTTOM ROW: W. JONES, T. LYNCH, NIPPY WILLIAMS, K. EVANS, (MASCOT), M. SCANLON, C. ROBINSON, P. HARRIS.

SWANSEA SENIOR A. F. L. PRESENTATION OF TROPHIES 1959-60.

BONYMAEN ATHLETIC PRESENTATION EVENING LATE 1950'S.

SWANSEA SENIOR LEAGUE V PEMBROKE LEAGUE 1959.
BACK L-R: B. NASH, RAY DAVIES, J. POPE, F. HOPPE, E. THOMAS, D. DEVONALD, RAYMOND DAVIES.
FRONT L-R: T. PHELPS, D. LEWIS (CAPT), G. RILEY, R. EVANS.

S. S. A. F. L. DANCE AT EMBASSY BALLROOM 1950'S.

SWANSEA SENIOR LEAGUE CUP DRAW MID 1950'S.
NOTE THE METHOD OF DRAW AND HAT.

SWANSEA SENIOR LEAGUE COUNCIL MEETING 1957.

MUMBLES ALBION A. F. C. CELEBRATING THEIR SENIOR CUP SUCCESS IN SEASON 1951-52.

SWANSEA LEAGUE PRESENTATIONS 1959.
MAKING THE PRESENTATIONS ARE MR. ABE FREEDMAN, PRESIDENT, AND MR. TREVOR MORRIS, MANAGER OF SWANSEA TOWN A. F. C.

SWANSEA SENIOR LEAGUE SENIOR AND YOUTH TEAMS MEET AT THE CENTRAL LIBRARY BEFORE LEAVING TO PLAY THE PEMBROKESHIRE LEAGUE IN 1958.

MERLIN ROVERS S. S. A. F. L. DIVISION 3 CHAMPIONS 1951-52.

PRESENTATION OF DIVISION 1 CHAMPIONSHIP TROPHY AND SENIOR CUP TO NORTH END CAPTAIN ROY THOMAS 1958-59.

GORS UNITED 1959-60.

SWANSEA SENIOR LEAGUE XI EARLY 1950'S.

JEFFREYS MOTORS CUP WINNERS 1953 BEAT U. K. CHEMICALS 4-1.
BACK ROW: FRED GABRIEL (SWANSEA SENIOR LEAGUE CHAIRMAN), G. JONES, G. B. JONES, P. JONES, L. GRIFFITHS, W. DAVIES, J. SULLIVAN, I. McFENTON.
FRONT ROW: R. THOMAS, C. JONES, B. HARRIS, V. DAVIES, D. MORRIS, T. ROBERTS.

UNIT COLTS 1958-59.
BACK: C. LLOYD, R. JOHN, D. JONES, T. MAUNDER, H. DAVIES, S. BURROWS.
FRONT: T. BENNET, D. BOWLES, A. EVANS (CAPT.), V. HELLYER, D. THOMAS.

CHAPTER 4 - THE SIXTIES

The 1960's opened with the promotion of the Swansea Town 'A' team to the Senior Division. Their side had progressed steadily through the divisions and gave the opportunity to a host of future League and indeed International players to start their careers. The teams were made up of lads on amateur or schoolboy forms, trialists and indeed young players who were already on contracts with the Swansea club. It gave these players opportunities which, would have otherwise been lacking in terms of competitive football. Apart from giving these lads opportunities, it was also a great chance for local teams to pit their talents against a team that was often called the 'All Stars'. To the Swansea League teams' credit they were often more than a match for their illustrious opponents.

A lot of people expressed the opinion that it was unfair for the Swansea Town 'A' side to participate in our League, the majority of opinion however, was that it was good for the standard of the League, and if one looks at the honours lists, the only successes they recorded were promotion to Division 1 in 1960, two Senior Cup wins in 1963 and 1964, and they were also Division 1 champions in 1963-64.

These relatively few successes gives strength to the argument that a lot of the Swansea League teams were more than a match for some very good Swansea Town 'A' sides. They played their home matches at Skewen Greyhound Stadium, where on a very big pitch they had the edge on fitness, but it was a different tale when they had to battle it out at places like Paradise Park, Maesteg Park or Ashleigh Road. All in all they were good for the League and many a player who made the grade at this time will tell you it was a good experience.

Perhaps the most famous of all those ex Swansea Town 'A' players to make the grade would be Georgio Chinaglia. This giant of a man went on to win many International caps for Italy and he would also star in the great New York Cosmos side which at the time included the legendary Pele.

Georgio also represented the Swansea League side when he made his debut against the Birmingham Works League representative side in 1965. The partnership between himself and Graham Newcombe up front paving the way for a very good win for the Swansea League side.

A special mention should be made of John Irving, manager of the Swans 'A' side for many years. John was quiet and a real gentleman, and quite a few of the players to come through at that time would pay tribute to him. After John left the position, John Pursey took over the reins, he would prove an excellent choice and the team continued to flourish.

Another side beginning to emerge at this time and who would go on to great things in the next two decades were the Unit Colts side, this team being the forerunner to the United side. The team entered the League in 1958 and was predominantly a works side, with the inclusion of one or two "outsiders". Under the guidance of Michael Hill and Glyn Evans, they made an immediate impact and were Division 6 champions in their first season. They then went on to win their divisional championships in the next two seasons, and then finished runners up in Division 2 in 1961-62 to take their place in the top division.

During this initial five year period, Unit Colts also took both the Maes-Y-Gollen and Gwalia cups, and perhaps their finest achievement of this early period was reaching the final of the West Wales Intermediate Cup in 1961, only to lose to a full strength Llanelli Welsh League side.

It was a remarkable start for the club, only for it all to change in season 1963-64. The Works Sports & Social section who were backing the side, insisted that if they were to continue their support, then

BI-ENNIAL REPRESENTATIVE MATCH

BIRMINGHAM & DISTRICT WORKS A.F.A. v SWANSEA SENIOR ASSOCIATION A.F.L.

SATURDAY 31st OCTOBER, 1964 KICK OFF 2-45.p.m.

T E A M S.

BIRMINGHAM & DISTRICT WORKS A.F.A.

COLOURS RED, BLUE, WHITE.

RIGHT — LEFT

R.G. KEELING
(A.E.I. Birlec Sports)

2. J. WATSON. (B,ham City Police)

3. V.E.J. TONKS (Capt) (Hamstead Colliery)

5 R.M. SHERWOOD (Mitchells & Butlers)

4. D.A. TAYLOR. (Bellis & Morcom)

6. S.D. JUKES. (Duport Industries)

8. R. MORGAN. (Lucas Gt. King St.)

10. C. BOHANNON. (Duport Industries)

7. B.W. BOULTON. (B,ham City Police)

9. J. BROOKES (Rover "Tyseley")

11. S. TURNER. (G.K.N. Screws & Fasteners)

Referee 5005 Mr. H.H.T. BOWN

Linesmen. 7718 Mr. J. WILLIAMS.
7892 Mr. J.L. GODFREY

11 S. NEWCOMBE (Capt) (Tower United)

9 C. CHINAGLIA (Swansea Town)

7. B. HUGHES (Winch Wen)

10 R. WALKER. (Cwmfelin)

8. P. JONES. (United Colts)

6. A. DAVIES. (Tower United)

4 B. JENKINS. (Brynawel)

3. D. LEWIS. (Unifloc)

5. C. THOMAS (N.D.L.B.)

2. J. LOYE. (North End United)

S. CROCKER. (United Colts)

LEFT — RIGHT.

SWANSEA SENIOR ASSOCIATION A.F.L.

COLOURS WHITE & GREEN

Today we welcome our friends of the Swansea Senior Association for the fifth time in post war years. Of the eight matches played each competition has been on the winning side on three occasions. The other two games being left drawn. A keen, interesting & sporting encounter is expected.

****

We acknowledge with grateful thanks the kindness of the Management of the Delta Group Athletic Club in placing their delightful enclosure, Club House, and other facilities at the Associations disposal.

****

N.B.

NO CHARGE HAS BEEN MADE FOR ENTRANCE TO TO-DAYS MATCH. STEWARDS WILL HOWEVER BRING ROUND TICKETS WHICH COULD WIN FOR YOU SOME £200. IN PRIZES AT ONE SHILLING EACH. BY PURCHASING SAME YOU WILL BE HELPING THE FUNDS OF THE ASSOCIATION.

"THANK YOU!"

SWANSEA TOWN 'A' 1963-64 DIVISION 1 CHAMPIONS. SENIOR CUP WINNERS.
BACL L-R: ALAN JONES, BRIAN BUCKLAND, GARY OWEN, COLIN PARK, COLIN HILL, JEFF THOMAS, WALLY POPHAM, ARTHUR WILLIAMS. FRONT L-R: JOHN HARRIS, PETER McCARTHY, TERRY JONES, JULIAN PHILLIPS, JOHN IRVINE (TEAM MANAGER), GIORGIO CHINAGLIA, JOHN ROBERTS.
KNEELING: BERNARD MORGAN, BILLY O'DONNELL, DAVID LAWRENCE.

UNIT COLTS 1960-61 DIV. 3 CHAMPIONS - GWALIA CUP WINNERS. RUNNERS UP WEST WALES INTER. CUP. L-R: P. JONES, T. BENNETT, T. MAUNDERS, A. EVANS, A. MAUNDERS, B. O'SHEA, C. THOMAS, G. DAVIES, D. RICHARDSON, R. JOHN, D. STERIO, B. ALLEN.

only members of the Works Sports section should play. This decision was rejected by the players and resulted in a breakaway. They decided that they would finance the side themselves and change the name to United, the new club being based at the Queens Arms.

The first season of the sixties saw Mr. Trevor Morris, Manager of Swansea Town, make a request to address the Council Meeting. He spoke at length about the qualities and organisation of the Swansea Senior League and highly praised its officers for the way they conducted their business. He said that he felt proud that his club were part of such an organisation and realised the part it played in his young players development. He told Council that quite a few young players had made the step up from the Swansea Town 'A' side in the local League and were now established first team players. He was also delighted that his youngsters were getting a good grounding in a very competitive league.

The Secretary Mr. Williams told Council that he felt that they should appoint a suitable person to provide some administration assistance for him as the workload was increasing with the League expanding and he said that an assistant would be invaluable. After advertising the position and subsequent interviews the post was offered to and accepted by Mr. Mike Hill, formerly Secretary of the Unit Colts. Mike carried out the duties for a short period and the position was then taken up by Mr. Walter Quick. Reference must be made here to the dedication of officials. It was reported that the League had received an apology of absence for its September 1960 meeting from Mr. A. R. Price. It was pointed out by the Secretary that this would be the first meeting that Mr. Price had missed in 25 YEARS. One has to have admiration for such officers, it is so easy to criticise League officials but when one realises such dedication it puts things into perspective.

MR. TREVOR MORRIS MANAGER OF SWANSEA TOWN ACCEPTING 3 TROPHIES WON BY SWANSEA TOWN 'A' SIDE 1963-64.

RAGGED SCHOOL A. F. C. (W. W. F. A. CUP WINNERS 1967-68)
Backrow (L-R) A. Thomas, C. Jones, D. Sharp, N. Miller, T. Cotton, J. Grenfell.
Frontrow (L-R) B. Ogle, E. Morgan, B. Martin, W. Fredrickson, R. Hart, C. Weaver

It was in the 1960-61 season that the League regretfully accepted the resignation of one of its oldest clubs when Ragged School informed the League that it could not continue to function. The League were then delighted, when in 1962 the Ragged School club, under the guidance of such people as Brian Myles, Dave Williams and Ernie Morgan, resurrected the club and thank goodness were back in business. Few people at the time would have realised that it was the birth of what would become one of the most successful clubs in the Swansea League. The rise of the club was phenomenal and by 1968 they became the first Swansea League side since the war to win the West Wales Intermediate Cup. It was a remarkable achievement and the exploits of Ragged School will appear in this history on many occasions, but in that sad episode in 1960 who would have thought that the club would have returned to such heights in such a short time.

In 1961 the league was rocked by the death of their long serving Secretary Mr. Bryn Williams. Mr. Williams had been Secretary of the Swansea League since 1935 and was regarded as one of the most respected administrators in Welsh football. He was a person who had given his life to the game and he would be greatly missed. Such was the respect and admiration for his devotion to the League that it was decided to set up a Memorial Fund so that a suitable tribute could be found to honour this great man. It was to be a Fund to which all clubs would gladly contribute, he was held in such esteem that the contributions would enable the League to achieve its wish to dedicate a marble commemorative plaque to the memory of Bryn, in the entrance hall of the King George Playing Fields pavilion, a most fitting honour for someone who had done so much for the Swansea League. The unveiling ceremony was carried out by the Vicar of Cockett, and in attendance were the League President Mr. Abe Freedman and the Chairman Mr. George Peters. A testimonial match in honour of Mr. Williams was also held at the Vetch Field in October 1962 when a Swansea League side which included five guests took on a Swansea Town side.

MR. BRYN WILLIAMS
SECRETARY S. S. A. F. L. 1935-1961

The League had to act quickly to replace Mr. Williams, and at a hastily arranged meeting of the League Council, the Asst. Secretary of many years standing informed them that he did not wish to be considered for the post. It was his opinion that the post should be offered to Mr. Quick and Council were evidently in full agreement deciding that the position be offered to him with immediate effect. Mr. Quick informed them that he would gladly accept and would endeavour to maintain the high standards set by the late Mr. Williams. Walter was an excellent administrator with a charming manner who also had a wealth of local football knowledge, so it was an ideal appointment. He quickly settled in and gave admirable service to the Swansea League until he resigned in 1968 to take up a coaching appointment with the Welsh F. A..

In January 1961 everyone connected with local football were overjoyed with the news that Mr. Billy Johns, Secretary and founder of the Mumbles Rangers club had been awarded the British Empire Medal in the New Years Honours list. If ever an honour was deserved then surely this was it. Billy being in a wheelchair for many years of his life had been instrumental in setting up and making the Mumbles Rangers club the fine institution that it has become over the last sixty years. It would take up most of this book to list the achievements of Billy, as he was a wonderful man and an inspiration to everyone not just in sporting terms. On February 14th 1962, came the news that Billy had passed away, just 33 years of age but someone who had put so much into his young life. It was a shock to everyone but Billy had left behind a legacy which is carried on today by a worthy band of his friends and followers.

UNVEILING OF COMMEMORATIVE PLAQUE AT KING GEORGE VI PLAYING FIELDS PAVILLION OCTOBER 1962 L-R: MR. ABE FREEDMAN (PRESIDENT), VICAR OF COCKETT, MRS. B. WILLIAMS, MR. GEORGE PETERS (CHAIRMAN).

SWANSEA SENIOR LEAGUE XI V SWANSEA TOWN BRYN WILLIAMS MEMORIAL MATCH AT VETCH FIELD 1962. BACK: B. THOMAS, J. THOMAS, J. LOYE, M. CROOK, S. GRIFFITHS, R. DAVIES. FRONT: G. NEWCOMBE, W. ABRAMSON, G. BRAIN, D. PEARSON, L. SHEFFIELD.

In 1963 the subject of a West Wales Premier League arose once again. This idea had been floating around for some time and has continued since then to be the subject of discussion every few years or so. The Swansea League were approached as to the possibilities of such a venture, but as no firm platform had ever been put forward the Council decided that a delegation from the League would attend an exploratory meeting that had been called. It is interesting to record that at this meeting in January 1964 only one club, Morristown Town, were represented, needless to say the idea, or perhaps lack of idea, was left in abeyance.

To show the relevance of inflation over the years could be easily highlighted by two examples from the early sixties. The first was that the League were told that they could purchase a full new football kit for the princely sum of just six pounds, it even sounded an incredible price to Council at the time. Further enquiries confirmed that this would be the most competitive price, so needless to say a new kit was purchased. The other relevant pointer was in September 1963 when the League were informed that the Cwmfelin Ground was being put up for sale at a price of £20,000.

The League were also asked whether they would consider the purchase. This ground, situated on Carmarthen Road on an area where the present MeccA Bingo Hall would be, was a top class playing area with soccer pitches and a cricket square and it also had excellent changing facilities. Looking back it would have made an outstanding investment and a home for the League, but Council decided at the time that such a venture as much as it would have liked it would have been way beyond the means of our organisation.

In March 1964 the League was shocked by the sudden death of its Chairman Mr. George Peters. George had been ill for some time but the news came as a blow to everyone. He had joined the League Council in the early fifties and had been an active member and friend to everyone who knew him. He was also heavily involved in community activities and also put in so much time with another of his loves, the Swansea Y. M. C. A. George would be missed by everyone and the League presented his

PARTY GIVEN FOR BILLY BY NEIGHBOURS, FRIENDS AND CLUB MEMBERS AFTER RECEIVING HIS M.B.E. *SOME OF THE PEOPLE IN THIS PHOTO ARE: MEL DAVIES, GEORGE JOHNS, LILLIAN JOHNS, MENDE MORGAN (VICE-CHAIRMAN), IAN BOYD, GORDON BOURNE (PRESIDENT), DOUG PEACHEY, MR. AND MRS. ALBERT PALMER, MR. AND MRS. G. DAVIES, MRS. BOWDEN, MRS. FURR, MRS. THOMAS, HELEN CLEMENT, HARRY LIBBY, BOB SMITH, JOE RUST, TREVOR 'CHICKY' MEREDITH, AND OF COURSE BILLY JOHNS.*

PRIME MINISTER

Personal and Confidential

Admiralty House
Whitehall, S.W.1

December 27, 1960.

Sir,

I have the honour to inform you that The Queen has been graciously pleased to approve the Prime Minister's recommendation that the Medal of the Order of the British Empire (B.E.M.) be awarded to you. Your name will therefore appear in the List of Honours to be published on December 31.

You will understand that this letter must be treated as strictly confidential until December 31.

I am, Sir,
Your obedient Servant,

T.J. Bligh.

Mr. W. Johns.

Letter from the Prime Minister

Press cutting . . . Evening Post, 14th February, 1962

Boys' Club leader dies, 33

MR. BILLY JOHNS, leader of the Mumbles Rangers Boys' Club, died today.

Although totally incapacitated and confined to a wheelchair, Mr. Johns ran no fewer than five football teams.

He died at his home in Higher West Cross Lane, Swansea.

He was 33.

His full name was William George Maurice Johns, and he was the son of Mr. and Mrs. George Johns.

He was a man of great courage in the face of the greatest physical adversity. He had a ready smile and an amazing capacity for making friends.

When he was honoured by the Queen with the British Empire Medal just over a year ago, Mumbles people shared his joy.

Billy Johns went to live at Mumbles from Swansea when he was a boy. His disability then was serious, but he was able to walk a little and he attended the Mumbles School, now the Oystermouth Secondary School, and later Dumbarton School.

VOLUNTEER

It was some years ago when his disability became more pronounced that a group of boys in the district volunteered to take him out in his invalid carriage.

Before long Billy Johns, from his carriage, had begun the organisation of those young friends into a boys' club.

Recently Mr. Johns had not been very well.

Councillor F. Mende Morgan expressed the general feeling of Mumbles people today when he told the "Evening Post:" "In spite of his great disability Billy Johns was a surprisingly cheerful, courageous and warm-hearted man.

"He will be greatly missed by the Boys' Club, for the boys really respected him and looked upon him with affection."

Evening Post Tribute

MR. GEORGE PETERS
LONG SERVING S. S. A. F. L. COUNCIL MEMBER. CHAIRMAN 1962-64

widow with an inscribed clock in memory of his work for the League.

It was also about this time that Council decided that it would provide mementoes to any player who represented the League on six occasions. It was a subject that had been discussed at many meetings but until now Council had always been against it. It was decided that any player who had played in six inter league matches would be presented with the League's blazer badge. It should also be remembered that the League only played perhaps one league fixture a season so the award would be for service over many seasons. The first recipients of these awards were as follows:-

John Pope (Brynmill)	1966
Colin Clement (North End)	1966
Lionel Kennedy (West End)	1966
Terry Loosemore (North End)	1968
Charles Leyshon (North End)	1969
John Doyle (North End)	1971
Michael Lenihan (S. B. C.)	1971

It was a fitting reward for all players who had given up their time and given excellent service to the League.

In April 1964, Mr. E. G. Williams resigned as Treasurer of the League. He had given many long years of service to this position and was standing down due to increasing work commitments. He made it quite clear at the time that he would still continue as an active member of both the League and with the West Wales F. A., League Council accepted his resignation but with deep regret. Council decided the Asst. Treasurer Mr. Alan Conibear would replace Mr. Williams and that they would advertise for a new assistant. The subsequent advertisement resulted in the League appointing Mr. Bob Kent, this was an inspired choice as Bob would go on to give many years of invaluable service to the League. It was also at this time that Council would decide that it would alter the structure of its Match Case committee. Up until now match cases had always been dealt with by the full Council, but with so many members debating each issue this meant that council meetings were so protracted that at times these cases overtook the need to discuss more urgent matters. It was unanimously decided that in future the Match Case committee would consist of four elected members who would sit with the Officers of the League, this newly formed Match Case committee would also be given full plenary powers.

One would find it hard to believe that it was only in 1965 that the provision of nets and corner flags on parks pitches was taken on board by the Parks Department. After numerous meetings with the Swansea Council it was resolved that for the duration of the 1965-66 season, the Swansea League would make a payment of £50 to the Council and they would provide goal nets on certain grounds. The sting in the tail was that the teams that were playing at these pitches would have the responsibility of putting up the nets and at the end of matches taking them down and putting them into the park storage area. This the Swansea League felt was a way of at least making progress in the continuing argument over the provision of nets. At the end of the season the League then felt that they would take it a step further and they decided that they would help out by purchasing twelve goal nets to supplement the ones that the Council owned, with the total cost of these twelve nets coming to £219. They decided that this money would be found by the proceeds of a raffle plus £2 from every club, although clubs who already owned their own nets would be charged £1. It must also be recorded that Swansea Town would make a donation of £50. It was only in the late 1960's that the Parks Department said that it would be responsible for purchasing and providing goal nets but pointed out that permit costs would rise as a result.

Earlier mention was made of the red ash pitch at Paradise Park. The League had been of the opinion for years that this pitch should not be used for competitive matches, and in 1967 the League were informed by the West Wales F. A. that this pitch was not to be used for any League or cup match. The pitch had served its purpose over the years but for some time the league had received numerous complaints regarding the venue and nasty injuries caused as a result of the surface, and they had in fact issued guidance to clubs some years previously to this effect.

At the start of the 1968-69 season the League was now running six divisions of twelve clubs each and three reserve divisions. We were now catering for almost 2,000 players and the League was expanding each year. It was during this season that the League were honoured when two of its players were awarded Welsh Amateur International caps. Richard Otten (United) and Tony Nancurvis (Hafod Bro.) were presented with framed pictures of themselves in honour of their great achievement.

At Easter in 1967, the League broke new ground when it was decided that they would tour Southern Ireland. The touring team was managed by Arthur Harris and Ivor Williams and including players, Council members and guests, 38 people made the trip. The tour took in two matches, on the Sunday the League drew 2-2 with Cork City whilst on the Monday they were unlucky to lose 2-1 to a very strong Cobh Rangers side. Both of the clubs played are members of the Republic of Ireland League which spoke volumes for the Leagues' performances. It was a very successful trip with first class venues and the hospitality incredible. One wonders why this contact was never maintained, perhaps with the sailing of the Cork Ferry from Swansea the link can be fostered again.

In February 1968 Walter Quick intimated that he would be stepping down as Secretary of the League. He informed Council that he would be taking up a coaching appointment with the Welsh F. A. and would sadly have to resign his position with the League. The post was duly advertised with many people showing interest, after interviewing all the candidates it was unanimously agreed that the position be offered to Colin John Ashford who duly accepted. How many members at the time realised that perhaps this was one of the most important decisions they would make as Colin went on to give almost thirty years of wonderful service to the League in the Secretary's role. Another decision affecting organised football in the area was taken at the end of the 1968-69 season when it was agreed by the West Wales F. A. that the Swansea Senior League could organise Sunday football within the Swansea district.

Because of a fire which damaged the centre stand at the Vetch Field the 1968 League Cup finals had to be played at the St. Helens rugby ground. This unfortunate occurrence meant that for the first time since the inception of the Swansea Town Football club the League had to play their finals outside of the Vetch Field.

In November 1969, two young lads playing football in Manselton Park came across a package which when opened was found to contain a sporting trophy. The two lads duly handed the package to the Central Police Station, they together with the help of Hubert Smith, a League committee man and landlord of the Dublin Arms, discovered it was one of the League's most prestigious trophies the Swans Nursery Cup. It was an important find by these two honest lads and the League duly rewarded them for diligence, who knows perhaps since then the lads might have played for and been part of a team that has won this trophy.

During season 1968-69 it became clear that further re-organisation of football was necessary in the

Swansea District. At a meeting at the Y. M. C. A. Swansea, on the 3rd July 1969, it was agreed by representatives of the West Wales F. A. and the Swansea Senior League, the Swansea Corinthian League and the Christ Church Friendly League, that football in Swansea would be administered as follows:-

A. Boys between the ages of 11 years and 14 years would play in the Christ Church Friendly League.
B. Youths between the ages of 14 years and 18 years at 1st September, to play in the Swansea Corinthian League.
C. All players over 18 years at 1st September to play in the Swansea Senior League.

The sixties without doubt, saw North End become the dominant force in the League. During this period they won the Division One championship on no less than six occasions, and in doing so they achieved two hat tricks of championships and also finished as runners up on another occasion. This feat of three consecutive Division One championships had only ever been achieved once previously, when Cwm Athletic won four consecutive Division 1 championships in seasons 1923-24, 1924-25, 1925-26 and 1926-27.

This was a very fine North End side of this period, at a time when the league was very strong. Such teams as United, Swansea Town 'A', St. Joseph's, Hafod Brotherhood, Port Tennant Stars and Tower were always in the hunt for honours, so it showed the strength of the North End club at this time.

The United side had now established themselves in the top division since winning promotion in 1963, and would by the end of the sixties become one of the most formidable teams in the area. They became the side everyone wanted to beat, as they made many shrewd signings and had an almost professional approach. At the time the legendary Harry Griffiths would remark that the side were possibly one of the most proficient amateur sides he had seen. Many keen observers would enthuse about their style, and they would refer to the goals of Jervis and Otten as a pointer to their success, but most of all would be lavish in their praise of the outstanding Phil Jones. Their best season without doubt was in 1968-69 when they won the League and Cup double, won the six-a-side tournament, and would also finish runners up in both the West Wales Cup when they lost to West End in a replay, and the South Wales & Mon. Cup where they were beaten by Hafod Brotherhood.

West End were another club who were beginning to make rapid progress at the time, re-entering the Swansea League in the 1965 season, they quickly made progress each year, winning promotion to the senior division in 1969-70.

Earlier mention has been made of Ragged School in this era. Not many people will realise that when winning the West Wales Amateur Cup in 1968, they were still a second division side, one wonders whether this feat had ever been achieved before in the cups history.

Between the two championship hat tricks of the North End club, it was pleasing to see the Division One championship go up the hill again, when in 1961-62 season Hillsborough would win the championship with Tower United finishing in second place. Tower went on to better this by winning the top division the following season. St. Joseph's would also achieve much success at this time, as they would win one championship and a runners up spot, whilst also winning the West Wales Amateur cup in season 1969-70.

Whilst Port Tennant Stars were always thereabouts in both cups and leagues, it was another East side club who were creating a lot of interest at the time. Kilvey Athletic had progressed through the divisions and made their debut in the top flight in the 1965-66 season. They were a fine footballing

UNITED A. F. C.
BACK L-R: J. HOSKINS, J. BIDDER, A. JOHN, J. JERVIS, D. HUBSCHMID, R. HOWELLS, D. OTTEN, M. HILL. FRONT: B. McGLYN, A. BEER, J. BEER, R. DAVIES, P. JONES, R. OTTEN, B. SAUNDERS.

side with many good players, three of the side, Laurie, Davies and Huntley, were ex Vetch Field staff who would give the side the added experience. Many good judges at the time rated them very highly and they were a force to be reckoned with.

Outside the top division at this time, the Swansea Boys Club were making rapid progress and since the 1965 season, had taken each division championship in their stride. They were proving to be a remarkable outfit and in this amazing run they set up an unbeaten run of 101 games. This record came to a halt when they were beaten 1-0 by Brunswick United in season 1969-70, the Brunswick goal coming from old stalwart Dicky Evans. It was an incredible run of unbeaten matches and one record that will stand for many years to come.

The sixties had seen quite a few changes, both in League Management terms and restructuring. The League was continuing to expand and was going from strength to strength and we had seen a vast improvement in both pitches and facilities, and with the co-operation of the Parks Department it was hoped that this trend would continue.

RECORD GOES AFTER 101 MATCHES

SWANSEA BOYS' CLUB, the Swansea Senior League team of the 60's, have lost their unbeaten league record—after 101 games.

And the player Boys' Club will never forget is Brunswick striker Dicky Evans. He ruined the record with a 60th minute goal which gave Brunswick a 1-0 second division win.

The fantastic string of successes started way back in 1965 when they rejoined the league. On their way to the top they picked up the championships of the third, fourth, fifth and sixth divisions and left opposing teams gasping with envy at their positive brand of football.

RIDING HIGH

Despite this setback they are still riding high as second division leaders, a position which makes them odds-on favourites for first grade soccer next season.

Brunswick, although overjoyed with the result, found time to give Boys' Club a few words of consolation. They conceded: " A draw would have been a fairer result."

REPRESENTATIVE MATCH

Hellenic League v. Swansea League

Witney Town F.C. Ground :: Sunday, May 12th, 1968

Kick-off 3.0 p.m.

HELLENIC LEAGUE Colours: Black and White

Right **D. BAXTER** (Morris Motors) *Left*

R. PERKINS (Amersham) **S. PELL** (Hazells)

R. BEESLEY (Bicester Town) **B. DISCOMBE** (Hazells) **R. TABOR** (Morris Motors)

C. TAYLOR (Marston Utd.) **R. DESNEULES** (Swindon Town)

G. HUBBARD (Swindon Town) **D. JOHNSTONE** (Amersham) **A. N. OTHER**

A. PHILLIPS (Plasmore) **J. PAYNE** (Swansea B.C.) **R. HART** (R. School)

A. N. OTHER **B. NUTTON** (North End)

R. OTTER (North End) **T. LOOSEMOORE** (North End) **M. SULLIVAN** (West End)

C. JONES (Brunswick) **J. DOLLARD** (St. Josephs)

Left **S. CROCKER** (United Colts) *Right*

SWANSEA LEAGUE Colours: White Shirts, Green Trim

ADMISSION BY PROGRAMME 1/6

NORTH END 1964-65 DIVISION ONE CHAMPIONS
BACK: C. BARRY, W. O'DONNELL, J. DOLLARD, H. DRAPER, C. LEYSHON.
FRONT: R. THOMAS, J. DOLLARD, T. PHELPS, T. THOMAS, A. THOMAS, E. THOMAS, J. LOYE.

ARTHUR HARRIS RECEIVING THE DIVISION 1 CHAMPIONSHIP TROPHY ON BEHALF OF TOWER UNITED, FROM PRESIDENT MR. ABE FREEDMAN, 1962-63 SEASON.

SWANSEA SENIOR LEAGUE XI 1963
BACK L-R: J. LOYE, T. BARROW, A. MAUNDERS, J. POPE, D. LEWIS, J. BOAT. FRONT: C. WATKINS T. PHELPS, J. LAURIE (CAPT.), G. PETERS (CHAIRMAN), G. RILEY, G. NEWCOMBE.

WELSH INTERNATIONAL RAY DANIELS MAKING THE SENIOR LEAGUE CUP DRAW 1960.

BRYNMELYN ROVERS INTERMEDIATE CUP WINNERS 1960 AT VETCH FIELD.
TEAM: D. DAVIES, R. SCREEN, D. MARTIN, I. JONES, B. O'ROURKE, T. HAMMETT, R. WHITE, J. MYLES, J. HUGHES, D. LONG, R. WILLIAMS, (MASCOT) G. HAMMETT.

KILVEY A. F. C. 1965
BACK L-R: R. FRAME, K. MARVELY, J. OWENS, J. MATHEWS, L. DOWRICK, A. LEWIS.
FRONT: T. TRACEY, R. BOYCE, A. LOWE, R. STEVENS, D. HOWARD, V. DAVIES.

SENIOR LEAGUE SECRETARY MR. WALTER QUICK PRESENTING LEAGUE TROPHY TO JOHN OWEN (CAPT.) AND HIS FELLOW KILVEY PLAYERS AT THE DOLPHIN HOTEL 1964-65 SEASON.

MUMBLES RANGERS A. F. C. 1960 SENIOR CUP FINAL, VETCH FIELD.
BACK L-R: B. SMITH, N. EDWARDS, T. JONES, D. AMER, E.WADE, D. DOWDLE, J. PICKARD, T. O'BRIEN, J. DAVIES, J. BUDGE.
FRONT: A. MARTIN, D. REES, D. SHEEHAN, G. RILEY, C. HENSON, C. MORRIS (REFEREE).

HAFOD BROTHERHOOD 1960-61
BACK: C. EDWARDS, J. HUGHES, H. DRAPER, D. GRIFFITHS, T. SULLIVAN, R. GREEN, R. GOUGH, J. JONES. FRONT: D. JENKINS, W. ABRAMSON, J. LOYE, A. DAVIES, K. JONES.

NORTH END A. F. C. DIVISION ONE CHAMPIONS 1965-66
BACK L-R: R. THOMAS, A. NORMAN, JOHN LOYE, C. CLEMENT, N. JONES, T. LOOSEMORE, C. JONES.
FRONT: C. BARRY, C. LEYSHON, A HAYWARD, J. BARRY (CHAIRMAN), T. THOMAS, J. REES, A. THOMAS.

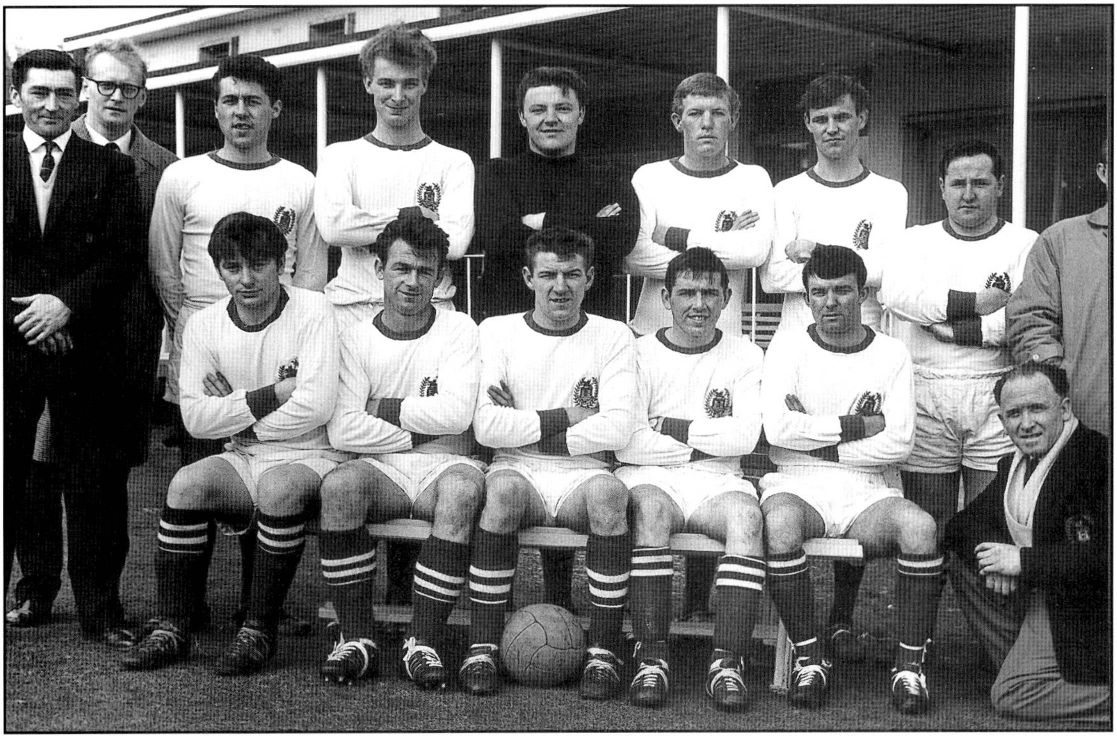

SWANSEA SENIOR A. F. L. V PEMBROKE LEAGUE AT R. T. B. GROUND 1965.
BACK L-R: J. COHEN, W. QUICK, J. COOZE, J. HARDING, S. CROCKER, T. LOOSEMORE, R. LLOYD, B. SHEA. FRONT: B. HUGHES, R. BEVAN, D. LEWIS (CAPT.), T. HARRIS, P. JONES, J. THOMAS (MANAGER).

STAR ATHLETIC S. S. L. DIVISION 3 CHAMPIONS 1967-68.
BACK L-R: CARL MORGAN, REG. ROWLAND, GWYN JONES, RANDY NEWTON, KERRY ROWLAND, JOHN HOOPS, MICKEY LENIHAN, KEITH ROWLAND, GEOFF DUNNE, BRIAN ALLEN, CLIVE HESLOP.
FRONT: PAUL KILLA, TERRY WEBB, JOHN HOPKINS, RON STUDDEN, TONY SMITH, A. N. OTHER.

PRESENTATION TO RETIRING TREASURER MR. EVAN WILLIAMS.

WEST END 1964-65.
BACK: C. LEWIS, J. HARDING, A AYERS, J. LEWIS, M. SMITH, A. WALTERS, T. HURLOW, D. SMITH.
FRONT: R. ROSS, R. PURNELL, R. REYNOLDS, G. MORRIS, L KENNEDY.

CHAPTER 5 - THE SEVENTIES

Further to the West Wales F. A. decision as regards to Sunday football, it was agreed that the Swansea Sunday Football League (a subsidiary league of the Senior League) would organise Sunday football and a division was formed for the 1970-71 season. It was always Mr. Ashford's view that Sunday football should be properly organised and come under the control of the Senior League.

It was the West Wales F. A. decision that the Sunday League should be run as a separate entity from the Senior League. Strong overtures were then made to overturn this decision and it was agreed in 1971, that Sunday football would no longer be run by a separate league, but by the full Swansea Senior League.

It is interesting to note Mr. Ashford's comments at the start of this Sunday venture. He said that it was too early to estimate the interest in such football. Perhaps this was an understatement seeing the progress of the League through the years.

In 1972, two divisions of the League were formed, with a Sunday Industrial division catering for industrial teams, and a Sunday division for pubs and clubs etc. The winners of the Industrial section for the first three years were Unit Sports, and it was in 1973-74 when the Swansea Docks side broke this sequence. In the Sunday division, Gatehouse recorded a hat trick of championships in the first four seasons.

It had been mentioned earlier that the League had always had the support of the Swansea Football Club. Since its inception the League had always had the Vetch Field available to them for their finals. It was in the 1971 season when the Directors of Swansea City A. F. C. refused, at very short notice, to allow the League to have use of their ground. Hurried arrangements had to be made, eventually the finals taking place at R. T. B. Landore, A. W. C. O. at Jersey Marine and at Ashleigh Road.

In 1972 all our finals were played at the St. Helens ground, with the refusal once again by the Vetch Field management to allow us to play there. An application had to be made to the Corporation Estates Department, asking for the use of St. Helens for our finals and they in turn put our case forward to the full Council meeting. Records show that it was only on the casting vote of the Chairman that saw our application successful.

History was then made when the Gwalia Cup final that year was held under floodlights, which was the first time ever for one of our finals. The Swansea League were hugely indebted to the Swansea City Council and the St. Helens groundstaff for all their help during this period of difficult relations with the Swans. Although relations were strained as a result of the refusal to loan the Vetch Field, subsequent talks ensured that the goodwill which had existed previously between the League and the Board of Directors, once again prevailed and all differences were resolved. This relationship has blossomed over the years and hopefully with the building of the new stadium at the Morfa this goodwill will continue and allow the league's finals to be held at the venue that fulfils the ambitions of every local team and player.

In April 1970 the League decided that in future, any Council member serving 21 years, would be presented with an inscribed memento. At the same time it was revealed that the League's Assistant Secretary , Mr. Arthur Price, had served as a Council member for over forty years, and therefore he should receive a suitable memento and also be made a life member of the League.

Another award made by the League at this time was a presentation to the ever popular St. Josephs and North End player Chuck Jones, this was on his gaining representative honours with the Welsh Amateur boxing team.

The end of the 1970 season saw United win the Senior Cup for the third successive year, whilst the League Secretary reported that we now had 2,146 registered players representing 71 clubs and 107 teams. The League was growing each season and it was beginning to show in the strength of the clubs. This would be borne out by the fact that by the 1972 season the League would have 2,642 players registered.

Chuck Jones

In 1970 the Munster League paid a first ever visit to Swansea, with the party sailing overnight from Cork and arriving in Swansea early on Saturday morning. They were met by the then Chairman John Budge and the Vice Chairman George Jones, and they were then taken on a bus tour of Swansea and the Gower Coast. They then proceeded to take on and beat the Swansea League team by 3 goals to 1, the match being played at the R. T. B. Landore ground. Both teams were then entertained at the Dublin Arms where they were able to watch the F. A. Cup Final on television. The Swansea League team for this match was:-
G. David (United), D. Lloyd (Tower), P. John (Waun Wen), A. Salmon (Port Tennant Stars), W. Popham (St. Joseph's), W. Greenslade (Tower), C. Jones (United), M. Sullivan (St. Joseph's), A. Thomas (Dublin), E. Phillips (West End), T. Jones (St. Joseph's).

The League team had better fortunes in their annual match against the Birmingham Works League in October 1971. They completely outplayed a very strong and fancied Birmingham side and were victorious by 2 goals to 0, once again the match being played at the R. T. B. Landore ground.

It is pleasing to record that the Birmingham League officials wrote to the League Council the following week to not only thank them for their hospitality, but were also very lavish in their praise for the Swansea League team. They also forwarded cuttings from the Birmingham Evening Mail which enthusiastically praised the performance of the Swansea League team, praise indeed.

The League side on the day was:-
J. Grey (Boys Club), A. Salmon (Port Tennant Stars), A. Davies (West End), L. Matthews (West End), A. Ayers (West End), T. Sillman (Rum Rangers), C. Thomas (Hafod Brotherhood), J. Doyle (North End), C. Leyshon (North End), M. Lenihan (Boys Club), J. Stephens (West End). B. James (Cwm Albion), replaced the injured Terry Sillman for the second half. When one remembers team selections for the best ever League side in the Evening Post in 1977, perhaps this side should have been selected en bloc.

While one almost always considers the likes of St. Josephs and Lady of Lourdes when reminiscing about Catholic Church sides in our League, it was pleasing to note that in 1972, another such side, St. Illtyds A. F. C., entered a side in our competition. They were valued members of our League for some

St. Illtyds A.F.C. Gwalia Cup Winners 1978.
Back Row (L-R) J. Harrington, T. Sterio, B. Ashford, Dan Harrington, V. Mullan, Den Harrington, P. Norman.
Front Row (L-R) W. Randell, H. Simons, D. Redmore, T. King, M. Lambert, R. Morris.

years and were winners of the Gwalia Cup in 1978. Then in 1982, the club changed its name to St. Thomas A. F. C. and were run from a different headquarters.

The St. Illtyds Club, under the name of The Shack, did make a comeback in the nineties as a member team of the Sunday section, but sadly, after a few very successful seasons, once again resigned from the League.

In April 1973, the League lost one of its oldest members with the death of Mr. Tom Day. He had joined Council after the second world war, was Chairman of the League in seasons 1951-52 and was one of our senior Life Members. Mr. Day had put in so much work for his beloved Welsh Juniors and for the League over many years and would be sadly missed. It is pleasing to record that his sons carried on the good work for Welsh Juniors for many years after his death.

In June 1973, the League agreed that in future they would change its policy as regards to the position of the League President. At a special Council meeting, it was unanimously agreed that the following criteria would apply to the position:-

1. The person appointed as President would be elected for a term of office for TWO YEARS only.

2. The person appointed would be the SENIOR active League Council member.

Most would agree that this new policy, still in existence today, would give reward to many members who have given many years of service to the League.

During any season, the League Secretary always has the worry of the elements, whether it be rain, snow or drought, but the latter end of season 1970-71 was hit by two other problems which one could not have readily envisaged. The first was strike by Post Office workers, as one can imagine this created havoc with the postal backlog. To add to this, there was also a strike of local Council employees, this meant that we were without Council pitches for our matches.

The Secretary Mr. Ashford, pointed out at the time that these strikes had caused what amounted to six weeks being taken out of the season. Once again it was only the ingenuity of our Secretary which enabled the League to complete its full schedule. West End would have been particularly pleased with the completion of the matches as their formidable side carried out the Double, winning the championship and Senior Cup.

In 1971, the West Wales F. A. conferred the honour of its Presidency to Mr. C. Marles, one of our League's Life Members. Mr. Marles had joined the Senior League in 1934 and held the position of Chairman in years 1946-48. This was at the time that the Senior League and the Gwalia League merged, Mr. Marles being a leading player in these negotiations. The Presidency of the W. W. F. A. was a very deserved honour for this fine administrator. Mr. Marles held the Presidency until his passing in 1974.

In 1972, Mr. Don Evans resigned as Assistant Secretary, and subsequently the position was advertised and was offered to and accepted by Mr. Len Williams. Len had refereed in the League for many years and was a very popular figure, but sadly he only remained in the position for a short time before being replaced by Mr. Len Davies. Mr. Davies spent many years in the post and provided the stability and efficiency the position needed.

1972 saw the West Wales F. A. celebrate its 50 years as a governing body, a dinner to celebrate the occasion was held at the Top Rank Suite in Swansea. The Chairman and Secretary, together with their wives, represented the Swansea League at this function.

At the same time it was also the Golden Jubilee season of Hafod Brotherhood, and as a prelude to this occasion, the Club won the West Wales Intermediate Cup, beating local rivals St. Josephs 1-0 at the Vetch Field. It was a great start to their celebrations and it is interesting to note that the following season they would again reach the West Wales final, though on this occasion they were beaten 1-0 by St. Josephs.

By a strange happy coincidence, in this their Golden Jubilee year, the Chairman of the Swansea Senior League was Mr. Evan Williams, a long serving player and official of the Hafod club. Evan was also a long serving member of the West Wales F. A. and past Chairman of the Association.

Many references to this great club will be written in this history of the League, they will all be fully justified and long may the club continue to flourish. The celebrations at the time included a re-union smoker evening and the major event, a Dinner Dance at the Top Rank Suite which was attended by more than 500 people, including Civic dignitaries, Vice Presidents and guests.

The League were to receive three extra trophies during the early seventies, firstly Hafod Brotherhood presented a trophy to the League in memory of Jackie (Blondie) Hughes, one of their former players who had passed away so suddenly. The trophy was to be played for annually as the Charity Shield match between the League champions and the Senior Cup winners.

Another trophy was presented by the Cwmfelin Social Club, this would be named the Fair Play Award, the winners each year being decided by the Referees Society. Last but by no means least, Mr. Jack McGillvary presented a trophy on behalf of West End Forge Ltd., this trophy to be used for one of

West Wales Cup Winners 1971 - 72
(Back) J. Bowen, T. Thomas, B. Stock, D. Griffiths, A. Edwards, J. Edwards, J. Davies, J. Rich.
(Front) D. Williams, C. Thomas, T. Jelf, B. Thornton, G. Davies.

President, members and guests at Golden Jubilee celebrations. Top Rank, Swansea. Season 1972 - 73

the Sunday Divisions.

Swansea City again refused the use of the Vetch Field for our Cup Finals in 1974. The fact that St. Helens was not available due to the early start of the cricket meant that once again the Secretary had to go cap in hand to obtain suitable local venues. Relations at the time with the Swans were at an all time low, in fact at the time, the Secretary informed Council that he did not want anymore to do with their officials. Gladly over the years, with different regimes becoming involved, has seen the coming together of both factions, this can only be good for the game in general and for local football.

Mention should be made at this time as to the help the League would obtain from various clubs in the area, clubs with private grounds who would always put their facilities at the Leagues' disposal. Clubs that readily come to mind were R. T. B. Landore, Aluminium Wire & Cable at Jersey Marine, Velindre Steel Works, Morriston and Pennard. These clubs and their officials helped the League many times during this period and indeed over the years, the League owe them a great debt.

On the subject of pitches, everyone connected with local football were delighted when in 1974, the Mynydd Newydd Playing Fields were officially opened. The City was desperate for a new complex and Mynydd Newydd has stood the League in good stead over the years.

Whilst we were enjoying the opening of this new complex, rumours were circulating the City that the King George Playing Fields at Ashleigh Road had been the subject of talks between the Hospital Management Board and the Swansea City Council. The first rumour circulating was that the Hospital Board wanted to take over a large area of the playing fields for a new Hospital development, secondly it was rumoured that part of the fields would be lost to provide a new roadway.

Letters were dispatched from the Senior League to our M. P.'s at the time, Messrs. Neil McBride and Alan Williams, and also to the Sports Council for Wales expressing our concern over both of the schemes. Replies were forthcoming from all parties and the League decided it would adopt a waiting brief. Obviously these must have been just rumours as Ashleigh Road has stood the test of time.

In September 1974, the League lost two of its long serving members with the deaths of Mr. C. Marles, who in 1971 had taken over the Presidency of the West Wales F. A., and Mr. A. Beal, a life member who had joined Council in 1951. Both members would be greatly missed. On a happier note, in the same month, Mr. Evan Williams, the League Chairman, presented a special memento to Mr. Arnold Williams who had completed 21 years of service to the League.

In the 1975 season, when the Swans were going through a very difficult period, it was decided to set up a Vetch Field Management Committee. The aim it seems was to provide the Club with more backing and would also give the opportunity for local businessmen and sporting organisations to provide this back up.

The Swansea Senior League were involved in the initial discussions and it was unanimously decided that one of our longest serving members, Mr. Evan Williams, would sit on this Management Committee. This was an inspired choice as Mr. Williams was one of the foremost administrators of local football in the West Wales area. He would provide an immense input to this new venture, and would also be in touch with the needs of what Swansea City could do for local sport.

Sadly it seems, this Committee didn't seem to have lasted too long, apart from the odd mention of the usual ritual of providing the Vetch for our local finals, one cannot seem to find any other worthwhile mention of this venture, so one must suppose it died a quiet death.

In October 1975, the League lost another of its oldest and most respected members with the death of Mr. G. McIntyre. Mr. McIntyre first joined the League Council in 1935 and had served in many capacities, being a past Chairman and President of both the Swansea League and the West Wales F. A., and was also a current life member. He was also part of the team that set up the Combined Services League which operated during the second world war, and for the eventual amalgamation of the Senior and Gwalia leagues just after the war. The League owes a great deal to Mr. McIntyre for all his efforts and love for the game over the forty years that he served.

Perhaps one of the biggest headaches for the League Council over the past 30 years has been the registration of Welsh League players participating in our League. Maybe one could say it has always been a problem, but because of events at the end of the 1975 season, League Council were unanimous that something had to be done to eliminate the situation whereby League teams, either seeking honours or avoiding relegation, played Welsh League players in vital end of season matches.

It had come to the notice of Council that one such side, attempting to avoid relegation, had used virtually a full Welsh League side to play in such a match. The rules at the time allowed any side to sign as many Welsh League players as they wished and to play them at any time during the season. Even though the club had not broken any rules, it was the unanimous decision of everyone concerned with local football, that this abuse was against the spirit of the game and that a rule change was inevitable. There was much discussion and recriminations at the time but it was agreed unanimously by Council that as from season 1976-77, any player who had signed Welsh League and Swansea League forms, would not be allowed to play for his Senior League club after the 1st March.

Over the years this rule has been adhered to and although there have been variations to dates etc., it has been applied successfully and the League has been better for it. This rule is still in existence, but a landmark decision in 1998, resulting in the West Wales F. A. having to take their case to arbitration, rocked all local football leagues, more about that in a later chapter.

The start of the 1976 season was delayed believe it or not by something that one would find it difficult to believe in this country - hard grounds caused by drought. Grounds had become rock hard due to a glorious summer so the local Council found it necessary to cancel games for virtually all September for fear of injuries to players and damage to the playing areas.

League Council members were reminded by the Secretary that this year was our 75th Anniversary and that we should be looking at ways to celebrate the occasion, to this effect a committee was set up to decide how we would celebrate the landmark. Reports from minutes at the time showed that early feelers put out to clubs had shown little interest. The League then took the decision to hold a 75 years Celebration Dinner at the Dragon Hotel on the 5th November 1976. It is pleasing to report that the Dinner was a huge success, and at a very pleasant evening, attended by Officers and representative clubs, local dignitaries and West Wales F. A. members when the following presentations were made:-

1. A Presidents Badge of Office from the West Wales F. A..

2. An inscribed gavel and base from Mr. Ivor Pursey for use by the League Chairman.

3. An inscribed memento from the Swansea Referees Society.

During the seventies, the League were fortunate to be able to call on four Football League Referees to officiate at games when available. All four referees had served their formative years in the Swansea League, and naturally the League were very proud to see them progress to such a level. The four, John

Gow, Tom Reyonlds, John Davies and Rhidian Harris, even though they had made it to the highest level, were still more than willing to spend their free Saturdays refereeing in our League.

John Gow in fact, refereed many international matches and top European games and he was it is true to say, one of the top referees in British football at the time. It was a shame that he was never honoured with an F. A. Cup Final.

One could write a book on local referees over the years, they play such an important part in our League and without them the League couldn't exist, but more on referees in a later chapter.

Once again in the late 1970's the League had problems obtaining the Vetch Field for our local finals. It was a great disappointment to all local clubs but the League again were grateful that we could once again rely on the usual helpful clubs such as A. W. C. O., R. T. B. Landore and Pennard.

It is always nice to hear of new pitches and facilities, so when the Secretary Mr. Ashford, attended a meeting of the Swansea Sports Council in February 1979, the news was pleasing. It was reported that a new sports complex was to be built on the site of the old Morfa tip. The venture would include:-

1. A bowl shaped stadium with a crowd capacity of 10,000.

2. A central ground - for prestige matches, e.g. Cup Finals, surrounded by an all weather athletics track.

3. Ample car parking facilities.

This was good news at the time because the League had another problem. Bad weather and industrial action by local Council workers meant that the League would struggle to complete the 1978-79 fixtures. Not only was the weather atrocious, but the industrial action by Council workers meant an overtime ban. This meant that grounds would not be available during this period but once again we found that Colin Ashford could work miracles, and, apart from the Sunday Division cups and the six-a-side competition, the League was able to complete all other matches.

In October 1979, came the shock news of the sudden death of Walter Quick. It was news that shocked everyone in the West Wales area as Walter was a schoolboy international footballer and subsequently had a very successful career in Welsh League football.

Walter was always a very good organiser, and it was this organisational skill that made him a Welsh F. A. staff coach when his footballing career finished. He was the Secretary of the Swansea Senior League between the years 1961-68, before resigning to take up his coaching post with the Welsh F. A.. He was also a long serving member of the West Wales F. A., and held the position of Chairman of the Association in the years 1976-78.

Everyone who knew or who had contact with him would agree that Walter was an out and out gentleman, someone who was always approachable and someone who had put so much into local football.

Walter Quick.
Secretary - S.S.A.F.L. 1961 - 1968

After the loss of Walter, it was good to record that the West Wales F. A. were making 40 year service awards to Swansea League stalwarts, Mr. Evan Williams and Mr. Tom Richards. The award was a new innovation of the Welsh F. A., its being meant that the first two recipients were local League members who had given so much to the local footballing community.

At the same time it was revealed that Mr. Evan Williams had been included on the short list for the prestigious Torch Trophy, awarded annually to a person who has contributed meritorious service to the community in the sporting sector. Nominations for this award are coveted, Mr. Williams' nomination brought delight to everyone in the area.

The award finally went to a Mr. Huw Harris (aged 87), who had spent 67 years in local football in the Cardiff area. He had been Secretary of his local club from 1912-46, and was then the Secretary of the Cardiff Corinthian League until 1978 before becoming Chairman of the said League. Mr. Williams when told, with his typical modesty said that "he had nothing but admiration for the successful candidate".

On the playing front, the early seasons of the seventies once again saw the United club the dominant force in the League. They continued their great run of the late sixties becoming Division 1 champions in 1973 and also finished in second spot on another occasion. They also followed up their hat trick of Senior Cup wins with another success in 1971-72, then the honours eluded them. Not many years after came the break up of this fine club, it was a sad ending and came as a surprise to everyone. There is not doubt that they will be remembered, for even in such a short history, they had enjoyed tremendous success and produced many fine teams.

Perhaps the team of the seventies was the Swansea Boys Club. Their record in the seventies alone saw them Division One champions no fewer than four times and finish runners up to West End on two other occasions. They were also Senior Cup finalists on three occasions and winners of the West Wales Intermediate Cup in seasons 1975-76 and 1978-79. In any standard of football it was a remarkable record and no more than this fine club deserved. It would also be a fitting tribute to all the hard work put in to the club over the years by the late Bernard Lee.

As was recorded earlier in the history, the West Wales Intermediate Cup had, until Ragged Schools success in 1968, become a bit of an albatross to the Senior League sides since the second world war. This was all to change. Since that landmark win by Ragged School, only one club outside the Swansea League up to the end of the seventies were successful in the competition, that was Fishguard Sports win over Hafod Brotherhood in the 1973-74 final.

In the seventies the successful Swansea sides in this competition were St. Josephs twice, North End, Hafod Brotherhood, Velindre Sports, Swansea Boys Club twice and West End twice. The dominance in this trophy would continue for the next two decades.

North End A.F.C
Back: J. Loye, T. Thomas, J Dollard, T. Phelps, C. Barry, E. Thomas
Front. A. Hayward, W. O'Donnell, Jim Dollard, P. Comley, C. Leyshon.

West End A.F.C. 1970 - 71, Division One and Senior Cup Winners.
Back (L-R) G. Finch, D. Williams, R. Pennock, D. Hubschmidt, P. Walsh, P. Ross.
Middle (L-R) R. Davies, D. Phillips, A. Bramhall, A. Ayers, R. Williams, P. McCarthy.
Front (L-R) A. Williams, J. Ash, J. Stephens, M. Smith, R. Richards, C. Hole, A. Davies.
Kneeling: C. Gilbert, T. Dawkins.

Swansea Boys Club, West Wales Cup Winners 1975-76
Back (L-R) R. Jones, B. Ellis, J. Gray, T. John, J. Morgan, M. Richards, M. Tompkins, T. Ayers, R. Richards.
Front (l_R) T. Leeworthy, P. Byrne, P. Newton, G. Roberts, T. Richards, S. Clark.

Plasmarl Senior Soccer Team

Port Tennant Stars, 25 year Anniversary Match , April 1972. Past v Present, Teams and Officials

North End, West Wales Inter Cup Winners, 1970 - 71
Back: T. Loosemore, T. Purcell, T. Thomas, C. Clement, R. Anderson, A. Couch

Youth Squad 1970's, with Captain Phil Evans and Coach Arthur Harris

St. Joseph's A.F.C.
Celebrating their successful 1971 - 72 season

St. Joseph's A.F.C. West Wales Inter Cup Runners Up 1972
Back (L-R) W. Poham, D. Tancock, W. Greenslade, R. Wilkes, J. Phillips, P. Powe, I. Aldron.
Front (L-R) L. Ford, B. Morgan, C. Jones (capt) A. Campbell, T. Jones, G. Newcombe.

CHAPTER 6 - THE EIGHTIES

It was decided at the start of the 1980-81 season that the Appeals Board, to which clubs in the League could use their right of appeal against decisions of the Senior League, was to be abolished. This Appeals Board, made up of three senior members of outside bodies, had been in existence since the early twenties. The West Wales F. A. suggested to the Swansea League that they give trial to a new system whereby clubs would appeal directly to the West Wales F. A., the clubs would then have the right of further appeal to the Welsh F. A.. The Swansea League took on board this new system which is still in effect to this day.

Concern was being expressed by Council members at this time that our old stalwart first aider, Andy Anderson, had been missed on the local parks. Enquiries revealed that Andy had now become a Vetch Field regular. Andy had been a fixture on our parks for years and had been a wonderful servant to the League, not only as a first aider but also a true supporter of local football. He was a gentleman and a friend to everyone. One would turn up for matches, particularly at Ashleigh Road, see Andy's presence and feel secure in the fact that expert help was at hand if needed. Andy had been an excellent sportsman in his own right, the family tradition being then carried on by his son Ray, who in turn was a fine player and represented the League side on many occasions.

The Swansea League has indeed been fortunate over the years as regards to first aid support. Not only have we been able to rely on Mr. Anderson but have been fortunate that three former fine footballers of our League have carried on the tradition. Terry Smith has been with St. Josephs all his life, player, committee man, manager and for many years in his role as medical support. Not only has Terry carried out his role for his club, but has also carried out these duties for the Leagues representative side. He has also been instrumental in setting up and running first aid courses to give the necessary training to clubs' first aiders. He is always available when asked to help, and many a club has been grateful to Terry when he has been called from his own game to attend an injured player. People have great respect for him and always talk about his smile and having time for everyone.

Mention must also be highlighted of the efforts of two former Port Tennant Stars players, Alan Salmon and Alan Bramhall. Both have given sterling service to their clubs and to the League team over the years. A bad leg injury has stopped Alan Salmon continuing of late, whilst Alan Bramhall has in the meantime seen service with both Swansea City and Haverfordwest, and has also opened his own practice. The League would thank all four loyal servants and all other first aiders who give up their time for what is an essential part of the game.

In April 1980, it was decided that the Corinthian League would become part of the Senior League. To this effect the Corinthian League's four active members would now become part of the Senior League Council. It was passed that Messrs. G. Cox, B. J. Bidder and L Buckland would become Vice Presidents whilst Mr. L. Thomas would be appointed a Council Member representing the Corinthian League.

At the end of the 1980 season Mr. Len Davies tendered his resignation as Assistant Secretary. He had held the position since 1972 and the League council reluctantly accepted his request, although Mr. Davies stressed that he would be continuing as a Council member. The position was subsequently advertised and two of the League Council members were interviewed, Mr. D. Savage and Mr. D. White, Council deciding that Mr. Savage be appointed.

The early years of the eighties again saw the League having problems obtaining the Vetch Field for its finals, once again local private grounds had to used and in the 1981-82 season all seven finals were played on parks pitches. There were at the time internal problems at the Vetch Field which would come to a head in the mid eighties, but again it was sad to see the lack of co-operation from the City club, this problem affecting our finals over quite a few seasons at the time.

In 1982 Mr. Bob Kent indicated that he would be standing down from his position as Treasurer of the League. Bob had given eighteen years service in this capacity and would be a hard act to follow. Not only had Bob carried out the duties of Treasurer but was also an active member and great support to the League in many other ways. He was a regular at all functions and an avid supporter of the League representative side whether it be at home or away. Bob would continue his membership with Council and as will be reported later in this history of the League, has continued to give that support through to the Millennium.

When the position was advertised it was unanimously agreed that the League would appoint Mr. Stuart McDonald, formerly the Secretary of Swansea Boys Club to take over this key position. This was an inspired choice for Stuart has provided tremendous service to the League and has continued the high standards of our former Treasurer. There is an amusing story which relates that when Stuart won a cup medal with the Boys Club in the late eighties, he was the only Treasurer in the history of the League to have done so.

1982-83 season saw the Hafod Brotherhood club celebrate its Diamond Jubilee. The club presented a Jubilee Brochure as a follow up to the Golden Jubilee one it produced in 1972. It was a splendid tribute to all that this great club stands for and has achieved over the years. The Senior League presented a memento to the Hafod club at their celebration dinner, long may the club flourish. It was also pleasing to note that at the time of their Jubilee season, one of their old youth team players, Jeff Hopkins, was appearing as a regular in the Fulham first team. He had also captained the Welsh under 18's and 21's side on his path to first team football.

It was also in this Jubilee season that the League and the Hafod club suffered a great loss with the death of Mr. Evan Williams. At the time of his death Mr. Williams was the League's longest active serving member. Evan joined the Hafod Brotherhood club as a player in 1925, and he was then the Secretary of the club for some twenty years. He became a member of the Senior League Council in 1935 and by a strange coincidence was the Chairman of the League during the Hafod clubs Golden Jubilee. He was also a long serving member and past Chairman of the West Wales F. A., and was also honoured by receiving the Welsh F. A. Long Service Medal. Evan had given wonderful service to football in the West Wales area, he was a first class administrator who was respected by everyone.

Other life members who passed away at this time were Mr. George Morgan who joined Council in 1959, and Mr. Jack Hackles who joined in 1962. Both men had given outstanding service to the League and would be sadly missed.

The League has always looked at ways at streamlining systems and in the mid eighties it was strongly felt that the Leagues' registration of whereby players procedure could be overhauled. There were many suggestions as to changing the then system, players would sign a registration form for each season and then become a free agent at the seasons end. He would then have to sign a new registration form for the same club, if he desired, for each subsequent season. It was a member of Council, John Hurley, who suggested that the League would be better served by using the system implemented by the Carmarthenshire League. This system meant that a player would sign for a club and stay registered with that same club until either a transfer or cancellation was requested. It was a far easier system to apply and although Council were of this opinion, it is interesting to note that it took them until 1989 to introduce this new procedure.

In season 1983-84 the Winch Wen club celebrated their Golden Jubilee, the club being formed in August 1933 when they entered the League Division Four as an under seventeen side. At the helm at the start of the club was Mr. David Maddick, 50 years on and David was still actively involved having served as Secretary of the club for some 36 years, retiring from that position in season 1969-70. He still continued to serve his club and the League, he really was an exceptional man. The club celebrated by playing a representative League side, the League responded by presenting a suitable memento to mark the occasion.

July 1984 saw the League being in the unique situation of providing both the Chairman, Mr. C. Ashford, and Vice Chairman, Mr. J.Budge, to serve the West Wales F. A. for a two year term of office. This was a great honour for the Swansea League, and it was also recognition for two fine administrators who had done so much for local football.

In 1984 there were feelers put out by the Secretary of the West Wales F. A. as regards to the formation of a West Wales League. It was his suggestion that this development would further enhance football in the West Wales area. Records show that all four local leagues were strongly opposed to such a suggestion. The Swansea League were of the opinion that local clubs were fully served by what their local league could offer, and were also of the opinion that the expenses incurred by such a venture would be beyond most clubs. It was also felt by most players that the amount of travelling, particularly those working on Saturday mornings, would make this a non starter and if they felt the need for advancement, then they could sign for a Welsh League club. In principle it was right of the Secretary to broach the idea, he was of the view that such a venture would eventually become a reality, but the support was not forthcoming and the idea was put into cold storage. The subject of such a league has arisen again in the nineties, but the local Leagues are still of the opinion that such a league is a non starter.

It was a sign of the times when in 1984, Council decided that such was the workload and advancement of technology, that computer and ancillary equipment would be purchased so that the League could keep abreast of the times. This was a major decision at the time, but when one looks at the further advancement of technology, mobile phones, fax machines, answering machines and such, then one realises that a League such as ours has to stay with the times. One wonders what Council at that time would have thought about the present systems in use, and especially the fact that one can now review the days results on television teletext.

1984 was also the year that Mr. David Maddick completed 50 years service with the Swansea League, it was an incredible milestone and people have to realise and admire what David has done for our League in virtually a lifetime of service. The Swansea League presented Mr. Maddick with an inscribed memento at a League Council meeting. It was also at this time that Mr. Arthur Harris was appointed to the position of Assistant Secretary of the West Wales F. A.. It was another role that Arthur would play in a long and dedicated service to local football.

This was also the year that we had to play all our cup finals at Ashleigh Road, as talks with the Vetch Field once again brought no fruition. It was pleasing to note that with the help of our Registration Secretary, Mr. David Savage, a then Director of Swansea City, we were able to hold all finals at the Vetch Field the following season. Records also show that the Sunday League section was flourishing, and we were now in the situation of running five divisions.

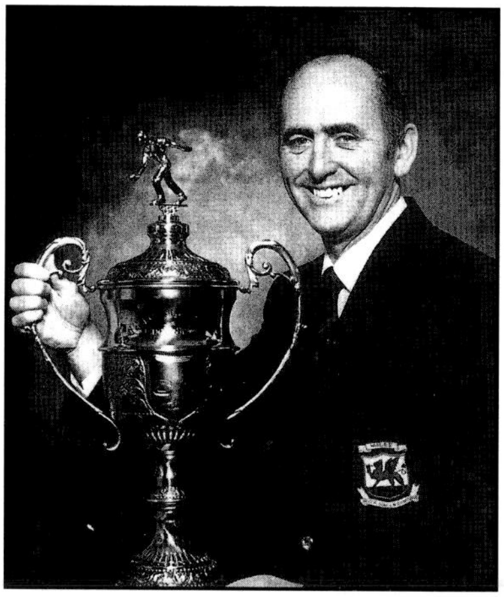

Terry Sullivan, 1985 World Indoor Bowls Champion

John Squires, British Indoor Bowls Champion

It was in the mid eighties that one of our former League players would be making the national news, albeit in a different sport, when Terry Sullivan, a former long serving player with Hafod Brotherhood, won the British Indoor Bowls title. Terry over the years has gone on to win many more major trophies and International honours, and going into the Millennium he is still one of the leading players on the Welsh bowls circuit. The League sent a congratulatory telegram to Terry at the time. In spite of all his success Terry is still the modest gentleman he has always been. Bowls seems to be the natural progression for our League players. Another former League player with Port Tennant Colts, John Squires, also won a British title, and one would be able to select a formidable soccer team from former players who are now very useful bowls players. Such players would include Dai Griffiths, Charles Leyshon, Roy Thomas, Eric Thomas (Hafod Brotherhood), Keith Beynon, Terry Purcell, Peter McCarthy (Cwmfelin), Ray Gough, Tom Crabbe (St. Gabriels), Dudley Lang, Terry Mills, Paul Bennett, Len Griffiths, John Beer (Morriston), Tony Phelps (Manselton), Alan Givelin (B. S. C. Landore), Terry King (Old Landorians), Archie Phillip, Paul Lucas, Len Barrow (Victoria), John Laurie (Dyfatty), more than enough talent here for a very good side.

The Swansea League has always been aware of the role that referees play, and it is perhaps fair to say that without them the League would struggle to survive. In 1985 closer links were forged with the Referees Society when Council took the unprecedented step of appointing a referees representative to sit on League Council. One of the League's former top referees, Mr. Terry East, being elected to this new position. Terry has held this position up to the present day and has been invaluable in maintaining the strong bond which the League has with its referees. Terry has also for many years served as the referees representative with the West Wales F. A.. The decision to appoint a referees officer was an inspired one, long may the strong bond be maintained.

In July 1985, Council first considered the possibility of seeking sponsorship of the Senior League. Such sponsorship deals at the time were rare but Council felt that the time could now be right. It was eventually decided the League would hold exploratory talks with Mr. David Allan, Managing Director of Exhuma Plant Hire, as to a possible deal. After many meetings it was jointly agreed that a three year sponsorship deal, for £1,000 per year, would start with immediate effect. It was also agreed that this initial deal would be subject to review from both sides each year. It was a deal that was most beneficial to the League, and Council would express its gratitude for the continued support of Exhuma Plant Hire over a period of six years, until such time that our present sponsors, Pic Up Spares went into partnership with the League. With the escalating costs of running a League, such sponsorship is vital for us to continue to give local football the continued platform to play on.

A special meeting of all League clubs was held on January 2nd 1986, at the Y. I. M. Club, with the meeting being called to discuss the plight of Swansea City Football Club. The meeting was addressed by two of its Directors, Mr. D. Savage and Mr. Bobby Jones, they appealed to all club representatives for support and donations to Swansea City 1986 Fund. They fully explained the precarious position at the Vetch Field and reported that all the Directors would be resigning at the season end. It was agreed at a later Council meeting that the League would support the fund by purchasing shares in the club.

For the 1986 season, it was agreed with the Parks Department that a new permit system would come into operation. The new system would mean that the Swansea League would become responsible for the issue and collection of monies from the clubs to the City Council. The League is now billed on a monthly basis, the system is suitable to all parties and would allow the League to allocate matches and pitches in advance, this being necessary to produce its monthly bulletins.

This year also saw the first ever finals at the Morfa Stadium. It has now become a common venue over the years but not overly popular to all spectators, the pitch being too far away from the viewing area. Another disappointment over the Morfa Stadium is the fact that the floodlighting is unsuitable for evening matches. This was surely something that should have been addressed from the outset and opening of the complex.

Jack Thomas

The League lost two of its stalwart members in 1986 with the deaths of Mr. Jack Thomas and Mr. Ken Grey. Jack first joined the League in 1948, he was past Chairman and also the manager of the League representative side for many years. He was also a long standing member of the West Wales F. A..

Ken was for many years a Junior League representative on League Council, he was also an excellent cricketer and had opened the bowling and captained the Swansea side for many years.

On a happier note, it was pleasing to record that Mr. Mal Bailey had been presented with a silver tray to mark his Life Membership of the League. It was a worthy presentation as Mal has done so much work for the Ragged School club and the League.

The League was also at this time presented with a new trophy by the Mumbles Rangers club, which would be in memory of one of their former stalwart members Alan Martin. The trophy was gladly accepted and would be played for at junior level football.

The 1987 season showed a worrying increase on the discipline front, with the West Wales F. A. informing the League that it had found it necessary to severely discipline a number of clubs due to the unruly behaviour of not only its players, but also its supporters. These clubs had been struck out of the Intermediate Cup and severely warned as to their future conduct. The Senior League responded by warning all clubs as to their responsibilities and that their future participation in the League would depend on their continued good behaviour.. The League has always been mindful of the need for good discipline and will always strive to maintain the highest standard for our League.

It was at the end of this season that Mr. Dave Savage tendered his resignation as Assistant Secretary. Work pressures meant that David could not continue to give the necessary time to the position. He had filled the role admirably for many years, and would be missed but would continue to serve on Council.

The position in turn was offered to Mr. Les Evans, and was a position he would accept and hold up to Mr. Ashford's death in 1996.

The League announced at this time that it would be making presentations to four of their long serving referees, namely Ken Wright, Mike Sullivan, Arthur Davies and Len Williams, the award being made for meritorious service to the League. It is to his great credit that, going into the new millennium, Ken is still one of the top referees in our League.

The Welsh F. A. also informed the League that 40 year long service awards were being made to Messrs. Glyn Bidder and Arthur Harris, both awards were fully merited and brought great pleasure to both their clubs and to the League.

On the subject of awards and referees, it was announced that John Holohan had been promoted to the Football League list, which was a justified honour for this splendid referee who holds the utmost respect of all clubs in the League.

It was early in 1987 when the Swansea Councils Sport and Recreation department met with the Swansea League and expressed a wish for all early Saturday games to start at twelve o'clock midday. They also said that they wished that all facilities for football at every Council venue to be closed by four thirty. They explained that they were trying to cut down on overtime payments and they felt that these suggestions would help in that direction. The Senior League had vastly different views however. The League Secretary made it perfectly clear that the twelve o'clock start for early matches was a non starter, he explained that with people working on Saturday mornings earning their living, that it would be impossible to both work and play at this time.

The Swansea Council took on board what had been explained and a compromise time of 12.45 pm was agreed on, much to the relief of everyone connected with local football. As most clubs would agree, with very little time stagger between matches, means that at some venues it is virtually impossible to gain access to a dressing room to enable clubs to make the later kick off time.

There is no doubt that kick off times in the League are a problem whilst we continue with the current situations at dressing rooms, and with the League ever expanding the situation could even escalate. Oh for the good old days when we were able to stagger our matches with a half hour gap between, this would alleviate any problems with overcrowding.

Part of the above problem was the reason that around this time the League set up a sub committee to look into the structure of the Swansea Senior League. Many members at the time were of the opinion that the League was perhaps too large and standards were suffering as a result. The terms of reference of this committee covered:-

a. Number of teams in the League.
b. Number of teams in the division.
c. Standard of play.

It was clearly felt by this committee that the League was, with the facilities that were at hand to us, at saturation point and that the present set up should be maintained. They also recommended that division sizes should remain unchanged. They also felt that any new club wishing to join the League should be 'vetted' by full Council. In the event of a vacancy and a new team being admitted, that team would not be allowed to obtain the transfer of any player from any other existing league club during their first season in membership. This would prevent a new club from transferring entire teams which would cause established clubs to fold.

On the subject of playing standards, it was clearly felt that the inclusion of Welsh League players for part of the season was having a detrimental effect and was not to the advantage of the League. It was the opinion of this committee that Welsh League players should be encouraged to compete fully in our League for the whole season. Not only would this assist in hopefully helping towards a raising of standards, but they could also assist in West Wales Cup competitions.

In the late eighties great concern was being expressed in the West Wales area as regards to the discipline of both clubs and spectators. There was no doubt that indiscipline was on the increase and the Swansea League were determined that they would take the necessary steps to combat this rise. To this effect Council passed a resolution thus, "The Council shall have the right to refuse admission to the League or terminate membership at any time, for any reason without redress. This right to be exercised whenever a Clubs playing or behaviour record is deemed not to be in accordance with the League standards, or if any Club do not accept its rules". It is an option that gladly the Council have not had to use, long may this be the case.

In 1989 the Welsh F. A. dropped another of its periodical bombshells on local football when they announced that they would be imposing a levy on all local players and referees. This levy they stated, would help to improve the finances of the Welsh F. A., and enable them to do more for the area associations. As shown over the years, they have come up with some incredible ideas, but this decision was even an embarrassment to the West Wales F. A.. They decided that they felt it necessary to pay this levy on behalf of its players and referees, also deciding to inform the Welsh F. A. that it would be taking advice from their legal representatives over any such further levy. The Swansea League also wrote to the Welsh F. A., offering many suggestions as to where they could make savings to eliminate the need to once again come down hard on local amateur clubs.

No one side dominated the eighties. Unlike the past few decades where the likes of North End, United and the Swansea Boys Club took the share of the honours, this seemed to be a more even mix and spread of the honours. In saying that the likes of North End, St. Josephs and West End were again to the fore but it was pleasing to see the emergence of other clubs who would come through and add their names to the honours board. The League would however see the demise of the United club and the failure of the Boys Club to add to their honours.

The eighties also saw the loss of one competition and another come to the fore. The annual six-a-side tournament which was inaugurated in 1963 finally came to an end in the 1980-81 season when Portmead defeated Port Tennant Colts in the final. More information on the six-a-side tournament can be found in a separate chapter and possibly the reasons for its ending. At roughly the same time as this competition ending, the League introduced the Open Cup for the 1980 season. This competition is open to all clubs in the League and would give the minnows a chance to take on the big boys. It has proved a great success and always throws up the odd surprise or two. The inaugural final in 1980 saw the West End club defeat St. Josephs.

The West Wales Intermediate Cup was again predominantly the Swansea League clubs possession, although it it did go outside the area with the victories of Suburbs and Trostre. What was unusual was the fact that the eight cup wins in this decade went to eight different Swansea clubs, and it was particularly pleasing to see new names such as Maltsters, Winch Wen and Port Tennant Colts on the list.

Ragged School continued to make progress and were once again successful in the W. W. F. A. Cup. They also won the Division One championship and Senior Cup on two occasions and performed the League and Cup double in 1984. West End then went one better when in 1983, they performed the unique treble of winning the W. W. F. A. Intermediate Cup as well as the Swansea League and Senior Cup, they would also add a further two championships and cup wins during the decade.

Perhaps special mention at this time should be made of two clubs, namely Blaenymaes and Maltsters. Both these clubs would, during the eighties, progress through the divisions and become more than a match for the top teams. Blaenymaes would have three Division One championships to show for their remarkable progress, they were also Senior Cup winners on two occasions and were double winners in 1988-89. Maltsters were another side who during the early eighties saw them make progress through the divisions, eventually winning promotion to the top flight in 1987-88 and the following season were runners up in both the League and Senior Cup. Perhaps even more remarkable was their achievement in the 1986-87 season when they won the W. W. F. A. Intermediate Cup whilst still a second division side, by doing this they had achieved what Ragged School had done in 1968.

Port Tennant Colts would be another club to win promotion to Division One during this period, they would also be successful in the West Wales Intermediate Cup in 1987-88, the same season as they won the Division One championship.

Mention must be made at this time of two clubs who perhaps hadn't appeared on the honours board very often. The now defunct Sketty Park Boys club would be successful in the 1985 Open Cup Final whilst the Mumbles Rangers club were runners up in the Senior Cup in 1987-88, they then followed this with a wonderful season in 1989-90 when they not only finished Division One runners up but won the prestigious Open Cup and Nursery Cup finals.

West End A.F.C. 1970's
Back: A. Davies, T. Walsh, M. Sullivan, G. David, L. Matthews, R. Arnold, J. Hill.
Front: D. McCaughtrie, R. Purnell, L. Kennedy, T. Sillman, J. Ash.

St. Joseph's A.F.C. Senior Cup Winners 1981
Back (L-R) J. Phillips, P. Mansell, D,. Fender, R. Pennock, P. Crane, R. Jenkins, C. John.
Front (L-R) J. Ash, S. Carroll, D. Tancock, W. Greenslade, M. Thomas, A. Campbell

St. Joseph's A.F.C Players and Officials celebrate their 1982 W.W.F.A. Intermediate Cup win when they defeated Johnston 3-1 at the Vetch Field.

THE TEAMS

RAGGED SCHOOL		ST. JOSEPHS
Mickey Walters	1	Ray Pennock
Michael Long	2	Alan Campbell
Gary Morris	3	Philip Crane
Chris Evans	4	Billy Greenslade
Nigel Griffiths	5	David Fender
Gary Newcombe	6	Donny Tancock
Keith Nelson	7	Shaun Carroll
Terry Purcell	8	Peter Mansel
Jeff Parry	9	Jaffa Ash 2
Tony Riberro 1	10	Michael Thomas
Kevin Hawks	11	Robert Jenkins 1
Paul Clarke	12	Colin John
Steven Beasley	Reserve	Ivor McCarley
Clive Brooks	Trainer	Terry Smith
Sid Foale	Team Manager	Julian Phillips
Ernie Morgan	Secretary	Colin Watts
Red with black shorts	Colours	White with green shorts
	Referee	
Peter Hooper	Steven Card	
	Linesman	D Wyn Williams

The Executive Council are very pleased to welcome you to the British Steel Sports Ground, Landore, for the Senior Cup Final and to thank the British Steel Management and Club Committee for their help in allowing the League the use of their facilities.

This final is a repeat of last seasons when Ragged School won a very thrilling encounter 3 - 2. St. Josephs will obviously be out to ensure that on this occasion the scores are reversed but Ragged will point to the fact that during league matches last year the Saints won both by the odd goal and this season history repeated itself with the Saints winning both their meetings by the same margin. Ragged School of course have done very well in this competition, winning in 1978, losing in 1979 and winning again in 1980 whilst St. Josephs, were losing finalists in 1977 and 1980.

Ragged School, although not doing too well in the First Division Competition have reached the Semi final of the West Wales Intermediate Cup and replay their drawn match with Portmead Colts (the side they defeated in the Senior Cup Semi final) at the beginning of May.

St. Josephs, have had a reasonable season and still have the opportunity of finishing in the runners up spot in the League Championship.

Both clubs are still in the Swansea Open Cup Competition and if both win their Third Round ties they have been drawn to meet each other in the Quarter Finals. St. Josephs will be all out to go one better in this Competition having been losing finalists last season.

Let us hope that both teams this evening put on a show worthy of their reputations.

Blaenymaes A.F.C.
Back (L-R) P. Davies, A, Williams, A. Templeton, A. Langley, C. Allen, K. Norwood, M. Debogarde.
Front. P. James, C. Sheehan, M. Vine, R. Pasqautino, D. John, R. Fox.

Maltsters Sports, West Wales Cup Winners 1986 - 87
Back Row (L-R) R. Woods, J. Mapstone, A. Wright, T. Kneath, N. Packard, D. Yates, D. Fender, G. Hammett, T. Leaworthy
Front Row (L-R) K. Nelson, T. Thomas, M. Hames, B. Yates, M. Berry, D. Paine, G. Newcombe.
Mascots T. Wright, S Nelson

Swansea Boys Club 1989 - 90
Back: J. Plamer, J. Scott, P. Jones, H. Lloyd, P. Sullivan, G. James, D. Jones (secretary)
Front: C. Lake, A. Riseley, P. Hopkins, M. Barter, I. Barnet, D. John.

Ynystawe A.F.C.
Back: H. Killa, G. Morgan, R. Evans, R. Williams, S. Jenkins, P. Foley, B. Cotton, R. Newton.
Front: G. Greenslade, R. Evans, R. Meredith, A. Sykes, M. Eaton, D. Packer.

CRC Rangers A.F.C.
Back: J. Williams, W. Davies, A. Crabtree, S. Ellis, P. Matthews, A. Davies, G. Hopkins, H. Owen.
Front: R. Rees, A. Turnbull, L. Richards, W. Bishop, P. Bennett, R. Ward, R. Russ, A. Payne

Mumbles Rangers A.F.C.
Back: C.Clement (ref) A. Reeves, M. Conibeer, D. Shervill, P. Crane, S. Tennant, S Harris, K. Graves, K. Billington
Front: A. Williams, A. Davies, A. Thomas, P. Reeves, R. Thomas, G. Morgan.

Dillwyn A.F.C.
Back: M. Matthews, S. Frances, D. Rodda, A. Thomas, K. Evans, G. Williams, B. Blades, L. Morgan
Front: J. Jones, P. Newcombe, C. Charles, L. Evans, P. Flynn

Cwmfelin Press A.F.C.
Back: J. Evans (manager) R. Otten (ref) J. Jones, P. Griffiths, P. James, M. Boyce, P. Hughes, J. Cornelius, S Thompson. Front: J. Thomas, D. Leeworthy, P. Jones, S. Thompson, C. Bevan

Malsters A.F.C.

Heathcliff A.F.C.
Back: T. Hicks, G. Adams, P. Barrow, B. Williams, G. Perkins, L. Matthews, P. Lynn, C. Hicks.
Front: T. Thomas, C. Grindle, T. Moss, A. Perkins, R. Davies, J. Thomas

Bonymaen A.F.C.
Back: K. Brookes, L. Alexander, N. Midwinter, P. Mansell, J. Szabo, P. Thomas, B. Jones.
Front: M. Thomas, D. Hurford, L. Arran, D. Vaughan, L. Frost, D. Hardwick

Bishopston A.F.C.
Back: G. James, G. Riley, M. Edwards, T. Lock, D. Male, I. Evans, J. Dixon, S. Peters, P. Catteroll, R. Jones.
Front: L. Woods, S. Kenny, K. Rees, D. Rees, C. Jones, I. Jones

Treboeth A.F.C.
Back: R. Smith, P. Siberry, P. Clement, M. Tucker, P. Rees, L. Restatter, K. Williams, D. Edgell, D. Smith, H. Davies
Front: S. Williams, C. Abrahams, C. Issac, T. Williams, M. Ferro, A Taylor.

Winch Wen A.F.C.
Back: G. Scrine, M. Mathews, N. Williams, G. Lewis, N. Scrine, K. Kenworthy, N. Evans, M. Glover, A. Watson
Front: K. James, S. Hoppe, P. Glover. A Robb, D. Williams, J. Lucas, N. Thomas

What a Season!
St. Josephs proudly display the fruits of a really successful campaign.

CHAPTER 7 - THE NINTIES

The nineties opened with what must rank as one of the finest ever performances by any Swansea Senior League team from any of its eras. It came with the Ragged School club winning the then Welsh Intermediate Cup.

This competition, one of the most prestigious of the Welsh F. A. calendar, was at the time open to all non-league football sides in Wales. It was a competition that always attracted a huge entry from North, Mid and South Wales clubs.

On their way to the semi-final, Ragged School saw off such clubs as Clydach United, Tondu Robins and Taffs Well, all three sides being from the Welsh League. In the quarter finals they then took on and disposed of Porthmadog, the then champions of the Welsh Alliance League, which meant a semi-final clash with one of the top non-league sides of that time, A. F. C. Cardiff.

Many sceptics were prophesying that this would be one mountain too many, but how many of the large crowd at Port Talbot will ever forget the wonderful performance of Ragged School against this very strong Cardiff side. It is also doubtful that anyone will forget the last minute winner from Simon Morse, which was a goal that deserved to win any game.

In the Final at the Vetch field, Porthcawl Town, winners of the South Wales Amateur League that season, were no match for a splendid Ragged School outfit who ran out easy 2-0 winners. They had achieved what many considered would be an impossible task, to win this prestigious competition, against the quality of teams that had started out some months earlier. No praise could be high enough for this very fine Ragged School club. Its players, officials and supporters had brought honour to the

Ragged School - Fan Trophy Winners 1990
back: S. Morse, C. Evans, N. Williams, D. Otten, R. Pasquatino, M. Baker, B. Donovan
front: G. Morris, P. Walker, B. Smitham, A. Thomas, T. Ribeiro, P. James, C. Sheenhan, J. Cornelius

club and everyone connected with the local league. In recognition of the honour, the Swansea Senior League presented the club with a silver salver.

In the same season, the club also won the Senior Cup and lost in the final of the Open Cup, whilst the reserve sides would win Divisions 2 and 3 of the league's reserve divisions. It was indeed an incredible season for the Ragged School club.

It was in 1990 that the Swansea City Council opened new pitches in the Ashland area, on the old Carbon Black site. The pitches and changing rooms being of an excellent quality, but the facilities were dogged by controversy since the opening. The problems have arisen due to the surrounding fence not being high enough to prevent footballs floating off into the adjoining bog, which again is overgrown with weeds.

An amusing match case arose in 1993, when it was alleged that the losing side in a cup match kicked five footballs over the fence and into the bog. There being no more balls available, the referee had no option but to abandon the match.

It is also widely rumoured that one of the local Port Tennant residents had a coracle type craft and he would pick up all the lost balls on the Monday after the weekend matches!

Such had been the furore from all the clubs playing there, that the League decided in 1995, that they would not list any more senior matches at the Ashlands, but they would make it available for junior games. It was a tragedy really to see two pitches, with excellent facilities, having to be ignored for the want of a suitable fence.

At the start of the 1996-97 season Kilvey Athletic decided that as their home pitch Maesteg Park was naturally given to more senior clubs, they would adopt Ashlands as their home venue. Whether the ground level or the water levels have dropped it is not known, but ball losses no longer seem to be a problem and Kilvey enjoy a playing surface second to none, with excellent drainage preventing a waterlogged pitch.

In August 1990, the Swansea Boys Club celebrated its Silver Jubilee, being the 25th Anniversary of the re-formation of the club. The original club had been in existence since the thirties, and had at one time played in both the Senior League and the Gwalia League.

It was in the 1950's when the Boys Club were particularly strong. They rejoined the League in 1952 and made rapid progress to reach the First Division. They were runners up in Division 1 in both 1954-55 and 1955-56, and achieved a hat trick of Senior Cup wins in seasons 1953-54, 1954-55 and 1955-56. Despite this record of success, the club unfortunately withdrew from the League in the late 1950's due to lack of support. Under the guidance of Bernard Lee however, the club re-entered the League in 1965, going on to what can only be described as a remarkable run of success. When they won the First Division title in 1970, they had won every championship from Division 6 to Division 1 in successive seasons, the only time this feat has ever been achieved.

The success continued throughout the seventies, the club winning four Division 1 championships and finishing as runners up on another three occasions. They would also win the West Wales Intermediate Cup on two occasions.

What better way to celebrate the Anniversary than by having a visit from Manchester United.

Even though it was a youthful side that would visit, it did include a young Ryan Giggs. It was a special occasion, and who would have thought then that eight years later, the Swansea Boys Club would fold through lack of support.

In February 1991, the League lost one of its longest serving members with the death of Mr. T. G. (Georgie) Jones. George had served with the League for over 30 years, as a member, Chairman and President, and was a Life Member of both the League and the West Wales F. A.. George was a member who was always out and about at matches, a popular man who always had a word for everyone. He was also, for many years the President of the Swansea Referees' Society, a position in which he took great pride. In his honour, his family presented a trophy to the League. A trophy, which is presented to a nominated referee each year for their services to local football.

T. G. Jones

Many meetings were taking place in 1993 between the local leagues and the Welsh F. A., regarding the Pyramid system being brought into Welsh football. It was eventually agreed that the Welsh F. A. would give the four local leagues in the West Wales area SENIOR LEAGUE FEEDER STATUS. This such status would allow the league champions of the four leagues, if they so wished and met with the criteria, to apply for Welsh League membership. If more than one team applied and met the criteria, then a suitable play-off system would ensue to decide the issue. In the event of the championship team not wishing to take up their option, then the runners up could, if meeting the criteria, apply in their place. Any such club taking up this option and playing in the Welsh League would automatically be returned to Senior League status in the event of being relegated.

In 1993, the League lost another of its long serving members with the death of Mr. Glyn Bidder. Glyn had been secretary of Cwmfelin Press for many years and had only recently been presented with his Football Association of Wales Long Service Medal for 40 years service. Glyn had also served as a member, Chairman and President of the Swansea Senior League and was a long serving member of the West Wales F. A..

At roughly the same time as Glyn's death, the League lost another of its former Chairmen and long serving members when Mr. Ben Jenkins passed away. Ben had joined the League committee in 1956 and had, like Glyn Bidder, given fine service to the League.

In August 1993, the Winch Wen club celebrated its Diamond Jubilee. Their association with the Arsenal Football Club enabled them to host this illustrious club to celebrate the occasion. At the time, Winch Wen presented two trophies to the League, one to be called the 'Jack Kelsey Memorial Trophy' in honour of this very fine sportsman.

Who would have thought at the time of these Diamond Jubilee celebrations, that six years later this famous club would fold. It was in November 1999 that the club informed the League that due to a shortage of players, the club was forced to sever its links with the Swansea Senior League. The club had been in existence since 1933 and it was with great regret that the League accepted their resignation. One hopes that perhaps in the future, the club could make a new start and recover its former glory.

It was at the end of season 1993 that Exuma Plant informed the League that they would not be renewing their sponsorship deal. Both parties had enjoyed a good few years of partnership and the League was disappointed to be parting company. Exuma Plant was warmly thanked for their years of sponsorship.

As one door closed another opened. Pic Up Spares, a successful local company showed interest in sponsoring the League and after many meetings with the Directors Tim Swain and Brendan Somerville, a sponsorship deal was agreed. It has been a very successful partnership, with both Tim and Brendan showing great interest in the League and participating in the many activities when approached. The Swansea Senior League is greatly indebted to Pic Up Spares and to Tim and Brendan, and it is hoped that this partnership will continue for many years to come.

In 1994, two of our Council members were honoured for their long and loyal service. The first, Mr. J. Budge was presented with the Football Association of Wales Long Service Medal for 40 years service, whilst Mr. L. Morgan was made a Life Member after serving on Council for 21 years.

John joined the Senior League Council in 1957 and has served as member, Chairman and President, and is the League's senior Life Member. He has also served as a West Wales F. A. member for many years and was Chairman of the Association in 1984-86 and is at present an active serving life member. John still gives everything to both associations, is a regular at all meetings and can be relied upon to give a calming influence to meetings when needed.

Les Morgan joined Council in 1972. He was actively involved with the Heathcliff F. C. for many years, where he and his brother Willie did so much to promote the club whilst in the League. Les was Chairman of the Swansea Senior League in 1982-84 seasons and has also been a long-standing member of the West Wales F A.. At present, Les is a Vice-President of the Association. Both these gentlemen fully deserve their honours.

In early 1995, the League lost one of its longest ever serving members with the death of Mr. D. Maddick. David was one of the founder members of the Winch Wen club from its inception in 1933 and served as Secretary for some 36 years. As written earlier, David was the rock on which the club was built and even though he had held office for some years, he continued to support and follow the club he loved.

D.W Maddick

Just a month later, Mr. W. G. R. Nedin, another of the Swansea League and the West Wales F. A. long serving members passed away. In the space of just one month, two of the area's influential members had left us and their passing would leave a great void in respect of local football. To perpetuate Mr. Nedin's memory, his family presented a trophy, the Ray Nedin Trophy, to be played for by the champions of the four leagues in the West Wales area, on an annual basis.

It was also in season 1995, that North End, one of the League's oldest and most successful clubs, informed Council that, subject to meeting all the criteria, they would be applying to join the Welsh Football League under the area feeder system. The Swansea Senior League enthusiastically welcomed the news, even if it meant losing one of our senior and most respected clubs.

What followed was not to be envisaged, and brought about an unwelcome and disappointing failure to the club's application. A local club had protested to the W. W. F. A. that the North End club had played an ineligible player against them, and, on appeal the case was found proven by the West Wales F. A.. This in turn meant that on investigation, the club had inadvertently played the said player in a number of other matches which resulted in the club being deducted a number of points. This deduction would mean that it would be impossible for the North End club to reach the first or even the second spot to meet the criteria of the feeder system. On appeal to the Welsh F. A., the decision confirmed that this would be the case. It was an unfortunate episode in the history of the League.

It was also a real hammer blow for all the work that this great club had put in over the years to achieve Welsh League status.

Just weeks after this episode, came the shock news of the death of the League Secretary, Mr. Colin Ashford. It is this sort of news that puts football into its proper perspective. A tribute and resume of Colin appears in a separate chapter of this history.

As anyone who knew the inner workings of the League would know, Colin's death threw the League into turmoil. We were between seasons at the time and this, added to the fact that Colin ran the show almost single-handed, meant that the Council would have a massive task in the short term to provide continuity. It is to everyone's credit that Council members rallied. This unity, coupled with the unbelievable support and inner knowledge of Colin's daughter Simone, meant the League would manage to steady the ship and complete all the necessary work, enabling the League to be in a position to start the new season in a way that Colin would have approved.

It is important to stress here, that without the support and unstinting help provided by Jean and Simone Ashford at the time, it was doubtful as to whether the League would have been in a position to start the new season on time. At what must have been a traumatic time for the family, both Jean and Simone provided not only all the League documents, paperwork and computer system, but also allowed officials of the League to use their home where all this necessary information was kept. The League was also indebted to the fact that Simone had, over the years, provided administration support to Colin. This knowledge coupled with the computer information, was the catalyst that enabled the League to continue as readily as it did. The Swansea Senior League was delighted with the fact that Simone accepted the post of Administration Officer and it is a role that she serves in a calm and efficient manner.

At an emergency meeting after Colin's death, it was unanimously agreed that the League should never again have the situation whereby the Secretary would be overburdened by controlling the League's affairs. To this end, it was agreed that the League would appoint a General Secretary, who would in turn, have the services of an Assistant Secretary who would take on board the registrations, as well as liaise and share the load. It was also decided that the League would appoint a Fixture Secretary, who would be responsible for all Saturday and Sunday divisions and cup matches. He would also be responsible for liaising with the Parks Department and the placement of all fixtures. Likewise, it was agreed, as stated previously, that Miss Ashford would be appointed as Administration Officer to provide support to all Officers.

League Council felt that this was the right way forward and the hard part now was finding the right persons for these positions. Mr. Les Evans, a long serving Assistant Secretary and someone who was fully au fait with the League and its workings, made himself available for the post of General Secretary and Council fully approved his selection. At the same time, Council approached and interviewed a former player, Club Secretary and Referee, Mr. Viv Nedin as to the post of Assistant Secretary/Referees Placement Officer. Mr. Nedin's application was successful and with the appointment of Mr. Terry Barbanti as Fixture Secretary it meant that the team was in place and ready to go.

It is to their credit that the League continues to thrive, and with Mr. David Habberfield now in position as Fixture Secretary, the structure is right and these Officers deserve praise for the way the Swansea Senior League continues to flourish.

Season 1996 -1997 started with the decision of the local Parks Department, that all the matches for the first three weeks of the season could not be played. This decision was due to the hardness of the parks pitches, caused by the very sunny and dry weather during the months of July and August. This was something new for the Fixture Secretary to take on board although it had happened once before in 1977.

On top of this, the League had another bombshell dropped on them. The Welsh F. A. making the decision that they would, for the foreseeable future, be playing all their Home International fixtures on a Saturday. They also decided that on the days of these matches, no local football could take place.

Everyone is well aware that over the years, the Welsh F. A. has made some incredulous decisions, but this was one that surely took the biscuit. Did they honestly believe that by banning all local football, local players and Officials would travel to either Cardiff or Wrexham for their matches? This decision has been made, without discussion and with scant regard to local football, and would further alienate the Welsh F. A. from grass roots football. All representations from local leagues were dismissed out of hand.

It was around this time that the 'one player one club' rule was being seriously touted to the Welsh F. A.. It was something that had been talked about over the years but now it was starting to gather pace. If this rule could be adopted it would mean that a player would, as professional players do, sign for a club and play all his football at that club. This would then eliminate all the anomalies caused by players signing for various clubs, and perhaps playing in three different leagues.

The situation is such, that some players are playing in the local Leagues, the Welsh League and the League of Wales. This is an absurdity, and if this new rule were to be brought in, would put an end to this farce. It is strongly felt that this rule will eventually come into force, in fact, at the Welsh tF. A. annual meeting in 1999, the vote was 51 - 38 against the change, this would show that the opinion throughout the local leagues is hardening.

Shortly after Mr. Ashford's death, Mr. Rob Kent, Managing Director of the House of Kent Ltd., kindly presented a new trophy to the League in honour of Colin. The trophy would be called the Colin Ashford Charity Shield'. It was a very kind gesture, with the House of Kent group also announcing that they would present a 'Man of the Match' award at every Charity Shield match.

It was in 1996, that one of the League's oldest clubs, St. Joseph's, celebrated its 75th Anniversary. The occasion was celebrated by various functions, but perhaps the highlight of the season was a friendly fixture between the St. Joseph's select XI against the Leeds United Ex-Players Association.

The Ex Leeds United squad carries out a great deal of work for charity. They were formed in 1977, when it was decided that by playing soccer games and organising other events, money could be raised for charity. Their selection was a charity local to their club - the Renal Unit at Leeds General Infirmary, the proceeds from such matches has provided much needed equipment for kidney sufferers. In addition, a great deal of money has been raised for other deserving charities. This Association has been a great advert for what such stars can put back into the game. The match at the Morfa Stadium was a huge success and it was fitting that a great professional club should provide the opposition for a great local club. St. Joseph's, founded in 1921, originally played their football in the Sunday Schools League, and have over the years produced many fine players, teams and officials. Perhaps more importantly, they have always produced a camaraderie and friendship, whilst winning every honour local football has to offer, and it has not been at a win at all costs policy.

Whilst the name of Jim McIntee will always be synonymous with the Saints, who will ever forget the work and efforts of the likes of Larry Cooney, Terry and Gerald Smith, Wally Popham and John Hurley. There are also many more who have put in so much work to enable the club to reach the 75 year landmark.

In October 1996, the West Wales F. A. informed the League that Mr. Bryn Bidder, Secretary of

Port Tennant Colts A. F. C. and President of the League, had been nominated to the Welsh F. A. to be put forward to receive one of the prestigious Torch Trophy awards. These awards are presented annually to people who have given dedicated service to their sport, and nominations are accepted for all sports throughout the entire British Isles.

The Welsh F. A. then confirmed that Bryn had been nominated for his long and distinguished service to football and he had in fact, been chosen to receive one of these Torch Trophies. It was news that delighted everyone, for if ever a man deserved such an honour it was Bryn.

Bryn has been involved with local football for some 46 years. He saw a need for an outlet for the local Eastside lads in the fifties and was instrumental in starting up the Crymlyn Burrows Y. C. to play in the Corinthian League. The club became very successful and as a result moved on and became the Port Tennant Colts side that we know today. The success that this club has enjoyed over the years can be attributed in the main to the dedication and drive that Bryn has given over the years. Eastside people will say that Bryn has given his life to the club, as Secretary, Treasurer, kit and laundry man, and to collect subs, book pitch permits, mark pitches and put up nets. Bryn, with the help of his loyal wife Pam, has done the lot. It is this devotion that has seen the Colts become one of the top teams in the West Wales area.

Bryn was presented with his Torch Trophy by the Princess Royal, at a ceremony at Simpsons in The Strand, London. His wife Pam and the long standing Chairman of the Colts, Alan Marney, accompanied him.

In October 1997, Bryn was blown from his bicycle and as a result, suffered serious head injuries. He was hospitalised for months but has made a remarkable recovery and is thankfully back in the old routine.

January 1997, saw the League set up a finance committee. This committee, apart from overseeing the League finances, would also strive to inject funds, to attempt to ease the burden on local league club finances. The League also took into account that with the impending Millennium and Centenary years approaching rapidly, this committee could provide a much needed back up, which would enable the League to celebrate these occasions with some style.

This was the year that saw the West Wales F. A., celebrate its 75th anniversary. The occasion was marked by a celebration dinner at the Brangwyn Hall in June 1997. This dinner being attended by members of the Welsh F. A., the Welsh League and all its member clubs in the West Wales area.

It was also at this time that Mr. John Budge, one of our Life Members, was presented with his Football Association of Wales Long Service Medal for 40 years service. The Swansea Senior League marked the occasion by presenting Mr. Budge with a silver salver, to celebrate the award and also to thank him for his service to local football.

For some years in the mid nineties, there was a concerted effort to set up an Under 17 and 18 division as part of the League structure. Many people had expressed concern that a lot of young players who, when coming out of under 16 football and perhaps not being ready for senior football, were being lost to the game. They felt that an under 17 or 18 division would provide an opportunity for these young players to bridge the gap and it would also give them the chance to gain the strength and confidence to make the step up to senior football. Numerous meetings have been held over the years, and each year the League has found that it couldn't obtain the necessary club support for such a venture. The League will continue to seek backing to make it possible to provide such divisions.

In February 1998, Mr. Len Davies received his Football association of Wales Long Service Medal for 40 years service. Len was the former Secretary of Waun Wen for many years and is a current life member and past Chairman of the League. He is also the Chairman elect of the West Wales F. A.. Len has held many positions within the Swansea Senior League, and his award delighted his colleagues who recognise the sterling work he has given the League. Also at this time, another of our League stalwarts, Mr. Les Morgan, was elected to become a Vice-President of the West Wales F. A.. This was a further honour for Les who is also a life member and past Chairman of the League.

As mentioned in earlier chapters, the issue of Welsh League players signing and playing in the local leagues has always been a contentious issue. The Swansea Senior League has always been of the opinion that it would NEVER stop players playing in the League as long as they accepted the rules and conditions of the Senior League.

As previously stated, the League for many years has had a rule which clearly states that: 'any player playing in a League NOT affiliated to the West Wales F. A., MUST if wanting to return to play in the Swansea Senior League, apply in writing and appear before League Council, before 1st December of that season'.

The League, when making this decision many years ago, felt that this date would give players the opportunity to determine their playing circumstances. It would also enable other players to judge whether they were capable of playing at a so called 'higher level'. The League also felt that this date would ensure fairness to all clubs in both league and cup competitions.

In 1998, this rule although ratified by both the West Wales F. A. and the Welsh F. A., was challenged, and on appeal to the Welsh F. A., the governing body ruled in favour of the club and player. The decision of the Welsh F. A. was against all that local leagues stood for, and this was demonstrated by the decision of the West Wales F. A. to challenge their findings at an Independent Arbitration Tribunal.

The West Wales F. A. were represented by the Secretary, Mr. R. Waygood, and their legal representative, Mr. Tim Jones. The West Wales F. A.'s case was most eloquently presented, and although the appeal was lost, the Chairman of the Tribunal said that he was of the opinion that the very ethics of local football were affected. He went on to say that he felt that the Welsh F. A. were wrong on certain issues of their case and, in his opinion, would have to change some of its rules.

It was felt by the West Wales representation, that the Association had won a partial victory, taking on board the Chairman's remarks, and this indeed seems to have been proven to be the case. The sad thing in this wholly unnecessary affair, was the fact that many thousands of pounds had to be spent by the Association to fight for what is the moral issue of local football. This money has had to come indirectly from the pockets of players in the West Wales area.

It doesn't seem so long ago that the pitches at the Morfa complex were opened, but in early 1999, a final decision was made as to the siting of the new stadium which will finally house both the Swansea City football and rugby clubs. The choice of the Morfa site was a surprise to no one, but it will obviously mean that one of our top local playing facilities would be lost.

In saying this, it is sad to report that for the twelve months preceding this decision, the League have decided that it would not be feasible to play matches at the complex. This is due to the access bridge, linking the pitches to the dressing rooms, being considered by the local Council, to be unfit for use. To continue to play at this venue, would mean teams changing in the dressing rooms and then either walking the mile journey or taking their cars the mile to the ground and then reversing the process after the match.

In discussions with the Parks Department, they came up with what can only be described as a laughable solution to the problem. They suggested that teams could change at the side of the pitches and leave their clothes on the touchline whilst playing. Obviously the Council's brainwave was not even discussed and other options were considered a no-go, so, for the want of a proper footbridge the Morfa facilities have not been used for league matches during this time.

The biggest concern for the League with regard to losing the Morfa complex was, where would the Swansea City Council be providing facilities to replace those being lost. Most people will realise that it takes some years to set up and be able to play on new pitches. It seemed at a meeting with the Swansea Council, that not a great deal of thought had gone into the matter.

Further meetings were held to discuss progress, and the Swansea Council informed the League that a new site would definitely be acquired. Many ideas were muted but the favourite option appeared to be a new complex on a site in the Swansea Vale area. In addition, they informed the League that they would also be building a new 700-seater stadium at the Swansea University complex. This pitch would have floodlights installed, the idea being that it could be used for cup finals and prestige matches. All local people, together with the local sporting fraternity, eagerly await the new Morfa development, but also just as importantly, the siting of the promised new football and cricket pitches.

Over the years, Swansea Senior League teams have had a tremendous record whilst playing in outside cup competitions. This record goes back to before the Second World War, when Swansea Nomads won the South Wales and Monmouthshire Cup, a feat they would achieve again in later years. Other Swansea teams to win this trophy have been United, and St. Joseph's, both these wins coming in the seventies.

In the West Wales Intermediate Cup, only on four occasions since 1968 has the trophy gone to clubs outside the Swansea Senior League. On three of those four occasions, Swansea clubs would lose in the final.

In the West Wales Senior Cup competition, there have been many fine victories by Swansea Senior League clubs over Welsh League opposition. Sometimes the margin of these victories has created severe embarrassment to these so-called 'elite clubs'. What causes annoyance over some of these cup upsets, is when Welsh League club officials and managers come up with the same old chestnut after being beaten by a League side. Their claim 'its only a one off game, you wouldn't last the pace in the Welsh League' wears a bit thin.

This bleat should surely have been rammed down their throats when, in 1990, Ragged School won the F. A. W. trophy, and on the way beat some of the top Welsh League sides in Wales. It was surely hammered home, when in 1999, Ragged School would win it for the second time. It was an incredible achievement for a local side and the League presented them with a suitable memento in recognition of their securing the trophy. Credit should also be given to their Manager, John

Now it's Swans turn to suffer a shocker

WEST End gave Swansea City a taste of their own giant-killing medicine by knocking them out of the West Wales Senior Cup third round.

The Pic-Up Spares Swansea League champions claimed a Football League scalp with a 3-2 victory at RTB Landore after Swansea's Jason Price was sent off after 30 minutes for a professional foul.

"Swansea played some nice football without really getting anywhere," explained West End secretary Tony Davies. "But we stuck at it and everything turned out perfect in the end."

West End opened the scoring after 15 minutes when a mix-up between Jason Jones and Price let in Wayne Jones.

Tony Bird headed home the equaliser 10 minutes later, but Swansea soon found themselves down to 10 men when Price was adjudged to have fouled Jeff Aspell when the striker was through on goal.

Aspell picked himself up to put West End 2-1 ahead from the penalty spot only for a defensive error five minutes from time to let Carl Mainwaring in for the equaliser.

After a fairly even second half, Aspell popped up again 10 minutes from time to knock Swansea out of the cup.

West End: Evans, Meacock, Mansell, Medwin, Brain, Jones, Hole, Fulford, Smitham, Aspell, Mark Sillman. Subs: Sullivan, Mike Sillman, Phillips.

Swansea City: Jones, Appleby, Bird, Casey, Clode, Jenkins, Mainwaring, Price, Phillips, Keegan, Barwood.

Cornelious, for how many managers can boast two F. A. W. trophy successes. Many a manager has been included in the Honours List for such an achievement.

To further emphasise the point, in January of 1999, West End would surely lay this myth of so called supremacy. They not only took on the Swansea City club in the quarter finals of the West Wales Senior Cup, but ran out convincing winners. It was an outstanding victory, against a City team, which included eight players with first team experience. It must surely rank as one of the best ever performances by one of our League sides. Sadly, in the next round West End would go out to a very good Llanelli side, but they had acquitted themselves well and had done the League proud.

In April 1999, the League was saddened by the death of one of its longest serving members, and surely one of its most famous characters, Mr. Arthur Harris. Arthur it seemed had been involved with local football forever. Everyone knew of him, and there is no denying that he put so much into the game in the Swansea and West Wales areas.

Arthur was totally committed to everything he did, playing in, as well as running the Tower United team for many years. It was a side that was one of the best in the area at the time. He was a long serving member of the League, and Chairman in seasons 1976-1978. He also served the West Wales F. A. for many years, being Chairman in 1980-82, and he played the role of Assistant Secretary for a long period.

Arthur was also, for many years actively involved in not only the West Wales Youth team, but managed the Senior League representative side on many occasions. Everyone knew Arthur, as he was larger than life and a loveable rogue, yet you would never hear anyone who did not have praise for all his work for local football.

To show how far technology has advanced, and how the League has taken advantage of it, is highlighted by the fact that the League match results, can now be scanned in the ITV Teletext monitor on a Saturday evening. Through the efforts of David Habberfield, our Fixture Secretary, it is now possible to read all the League's results, simply by tuning into ITV Teletext and turning to page 477.

What would some of our early day secretaries have made of all this. One would suppose that in their day, perhaps the only way to find out other results was possibly a chance meeting with players from other clubs. Nevertheless, it is progress, and the League realises that to maintain our high standards, we have to keep abreast of such technology.

It had been hoped that the Arbitration Tribunal decision, as regards to the Welsh F. A. Rule 52, had settled any future debate or anomalies, once and for all. Not so it appears. The Welsh F. A. interpretation and stance has not changed, and as a result the League has, for the past two seasons, put the Sunday Senior Cup on hold. It is an unfair situation, not only for those who have battled their way to the semi-final stages, but also for the very fabric of the game at local level.

In early 2000, the subject has one again reared its ugly head. The Welsh F. A. have made it perfectly clear that their stance as regards to Rule 52, is as rigid as ever. They, and the Welsh League must surely realise soon, that opinion at grass roots level is gathering pace, and eventually might force these people to realise that the present ludicrous policy, as regards to Rule 52, must be brought to an end.

In January 2000, it came to the notice of the League, that representations were being made to take over one of the football pitches at Ashleigh Road playing fields. In spite of many meetings between the Swansea City Council and the Swansea Senior League on other matters, no mention had ever been made of the proposed take-over of this football pitch. It only came to light when a notice appeared in the local press, giving notice of the proposal, and inviting objections to the proposed scheme to be sent to the Council's legal department.

Swans shocked as West End spring surprise

West End 2
Swansea City 0

WEST End produced another giant-killing performance to knock Swansea City out of the West Wales Senior Cup at RTB Landore.

Second-half goals from Jeff Aspell and Leighton Morgan earned the Swansea League side a repeat of last season's third-round victory.

Swansea named a young, but experienced side that included the likes of Tony Bird, Stuart Roberts, Michael Keegan, Ryan Casey and Tommy Mutton.

They suffered a setback just before the interval when goalkeeper Carl Thomas was forced to leave the field with a broken finger.

But after an even first half where Bird forced Cliff Evans into a good save, it was the local league side who took the lead 10 minutes after the break.

Neil Phillips delivered a deep corner to the edge of the six yard box and Jeff Aspell swept the ball home.

The Pic-Up Spares Swansea League champions clinched victory 10 minutes from time when Leighton Morgan unleashed a superb 25-yard shot which dipped under the bar.

"We just didn't give Swansea chance to settle," explained West End secretary Tony Davies. "We didn't allow them to play.

"After last season's victory we didn't know whether we could repeat the feat, but all the hard work paid off. It was a good game and I think we deserved the victory."

It transpires, that due to the fact that the City were to acquire an Olympic size 50 metre swimming pool, to be built at the University complex, then the council would need this pitch to replace the tennis court facility. The League fully realise that the building of this pool is a major coup for the City of Swansea, but what they seriously object to, is that the City Council would not even have the courtesy to discuss the proposal with them.

It has long been the wish of the Swansea Senior League to have closer links with the City Council, and when one realises that the League pour £70,000 per season into permit costs, then their treatment in the handling of this project leaves a lot to be desired.

The dawn of the new Millennium has brought home the fact that our Centenary Year is almost with us. When some years ago it was casually mentioned in meetings, the feeling seemed to be that we would have plenty of time to think about its implications. Time has flown and many people have since put in long hours of work, to ensure that the landmark will be celebrated in a manner it deserves. Many events are being arranged including, a celebrity dinner at the Brangwyn Hall, and a players evening at the same venue, also matches against Swansea City and at least one Premiership club, are just a few of the occasions planned.

When West End defeated Swansea City in early 1999, some people still had doubts about the strength of local sides, and what better way to destroy those doubts than to go out and do it all again. In January 2000, West End again drew Swansea City in the third round of the West Wales Senior Cup, again the venue being the R. T. B. Ground at Landore. Again the Swans fielded a very experienced side, but once again were no match for the local League side. Second half goals from Jeff Aspell and Leighton Morgan earned the Swansea League side a tremendous repeat of last season's third round victory. It was a thoroughly deserved win, and once again showed the West End club to be one of the foremost sides in the area.

On the playing side, the highlight would undoubtedly be the winning of the F. A. W. Trophy, on two occasions by the Ragged School club. Most clubs in Wales would give anything to get their names on the trophy, but to do it twice in nine seasons was a remarkable achievement for a local amateur side.

These victories have been highlighted earlier, but what it does show is the high standard of teams in our League. It is also something that everyone connected with local football should be proud of.

On the League and Cup front, two teams have undoubtedly dominated the awards. The Ragged School and West End clubs have almost had a monopoly of the honours, during the nineties.

Apart from their two F. A. W. Trophy wins, the Ragged School club has been successful in winning two Division 1 championships, and has also finished runners up on another two occasions. In the Senior Cup, they have had even more success, having won the trophy on four occasions, including a hat trick of cup wins in seasons 1990-91, 1991-92 and 1992-93. In addition to this, they were also to win the West Wales Intermediate Cup three times during this period, a remarkable record for this fine club. It doesn't end there either, as they have also won the Open Cup on no fewer than five occasions. Their success in this competition included a hat trick of wins in the first three seasons of the decade.

It has been an incredible ten years for the Ragged School club. Their level of achievement has been the reward for all the hard work put in by a dedicated bunch of players and officials. Their success has brought great honour to the League and provided many exciting moments, not only for their supporters, but also for all local followers of the game.

West End has also been a domineering force in the nineties. Like Ragged School, their list of successes is just as impressive. There is little doubt, that these two clubs have dominated not only the League and Cup honours, but have also emerged as the top teams in the West Wales area.

West End, superbly marshalled by the legendary Donny Smitham, have reaped the benefits of their excellent youth policy. For some years now, the club has produced some outstanding young players who have also been given the chance to play at a higher level. The policy has been proven and the club has enjoyed enormous success with a very young side.

The West End club has won the Division 1 championship on the last four occasions, and during this period, they have dominated the division and it will take a very good side to take it away from them. They have also finished as runners up on another two occasions. These statistics would show the strength that they maintain in this division. West End has also been hugely successful in the Cup competitions, having won the Senior Cup, Open Cup and the West Wales Intermediate Cup on two occasions each. Similarly, they have been losing finalists in the three competitions a further twice.

Perhaps to further emphasise the point of youngsters coming through, one should note that not only have the West End club won the last four Division 1 titles, but their reserve team has also won the reserve Division 1 title at the same time.

Whilst the two teams have dominated the nineties, several other clubs have been among the major honours, giving emphasis that the strength of the League is not just confined to these clubs. Port

Tennant Colts and North End have both had Division 1 championship successes during this period and they both also have Senior, Open and West Wales Cup honours to further emphasise the point. Meanwhile, St. Joseph's seemed to be the perennial runners up in both the League and Cup competitions. Even so, the club has proved that it has established a sound base, and is a match for anyone on their day.

In the mid nineties, two new names came into prominence. Both Treboeth and Brunswick would show how far they had advanced, by each winning the West Wales Intermediate Cup. In 1995, Treboeth were beaten in the Final by the Ragged School club and they then went one better the following season, beating local rivals St. Joseph's, in the final. It was sad, that just a season after winning the West Wales Cup, Treboeth lost most of its players to other clubs and were forced to struggle for a while. Thankfully the club is now booming again and looking for a quick return to the top flight.

Brunswick at this time was also a strong outfit. This was proved by their epic West Wales Cup Final win over the highly rated favourites, West End. Who will ever forget the match, with the clubs still locked together after extra time, Brunswick eventually going through 11-10 after penalties.

A deserved mention must be made of the performance of the Swansea Boys Club Veterans XI. The club found it necessary to resign from the League some years ago, the clubs older players have kept together and for some years have entered the Umbro Veterans Trophy. In 1999, the club played well and were fortunate to reach the final. This meant a trip to what every footballer dreams about, whether amateur or professional, a final at Wembley Stadium. Even though the club was beaten in the final, it had been a tremendous experience, which once again showed the strength of local football, even at the veteran stage. Well done lads

Swansea Boys Club
Umbro Veterans finalists at Wembley Stadium 1999.

The end of the decade brought in the new Millennium. The last ten years had been a successful period and had continued to see the League flourish. Although the death of Colin Ashford had been a great loss, and one, which we struggled to come to terms with, we can only look forward with anticipation. We also look forward to see whether other clubs could break the recent domination of the West End club as regards to the Division One championship, and whether one of our clubs could hopefully regain the West Wales Intermediate Cup, which deservedly went to the very fine Hakin United side in 1999.

Both questions would be answered with a positive affirmative, but the end of seasons happenings were perhaps not what everyone's predictions might have been.

The four year reign of West End's Division One championship dominance came to an end, when the Ragged School club, with a wonderful run of victories in the late season, and with a 4-1 victory over West End in their penultimate match of the season, meant that the club only needed a draw from their last match with Port Tennant Colts to win the championship. Seal it they did with another win, and it brought them their first Division One championship for some years. It was a wonderful achievement for this fine club.

To add to this, and by a strange coincidence, both the Ragged School and West End clubs were ultimately to face each other in both the Open Cup and Senior Cup finals. Once again the Ragged School club were victorious on both occasions, winning the Open Cup 9-8 on penalties after a 2-2 draw, and the Senior Cup by 4 goals to 2. Both finals were very evenly contested and illustrated the high standards set by these very fine clubs.

It had been an incredible season for Ragged School to achieve this magnificent treble. Praise must go to John Cornelius and his coaching team, the players and the equally loyal bunch of club officials.

When the W. W. F. A. Intermediate Cup went out of our League clubs possession in 1999, great thought was given as to which Swansea League team would win it back. What would have been the odds given by the bookmakers on Second Division side Mountain Dew Rovers being that club. After some excellent victories in the earlier rounds, the Mount then disposed of highly fancied Port Tennant Colts in the semi-final at Ammanford, winning by 2 goals to 1. In the final at the Vetch Field, they once again defied all the odds to defeat the much rated Goodwick United side by the single goal to achieve a fairy tale victory and return the cup to Swansea.

It was a romantic and highly popular achievement, and once again great credit is due to the players, supporters, officials and perhaps above all the reward for the efforts of the club secretary Steve Hammett, fully deserves. It was a success that not only Steve would have enjoyed but one that he would gladly attribute and share with his dad, the late Tommy Hammett.

Ragged School A.F.C celebrate after their West Wales F.A Cup win at the Vetch Field April 1993.

Johnny Jones, Captain Port Tennant Colts, receives the Senior Cup from Brendan Somerville, director of league sponsors Pic Up Spares Ltd at Vetch Field 1993-94.

Chris Evans, Captain Ragged School A.F.C receiving the West Wales F.A Cup from Mr Glyn Jones at the Vetch Field 1990.

Colin Miller (Mountain Dew A.F.C) receives his Golden Boot Award from Bob Waygood, secretary West Wales F.A.

West End Captain Donny Smitham proudly holds the W.W.F.A Cup. 1997-98 season.

Brunswick United – W.W.F.A Cup winners 1996-97.
Standing (L-R): *R.Lynn, M.Wheeler, J.Lancy (manager), I. Hellyer, P.Wheeler, W.Hyett, D.Beniamous, A.Ley.*
Kneeling (L-R): *J.Price, J.Orme, J.Corey, P.Brooks, C.Wheeler, J.Angos, S.Miles.*

Alex Milne (Bishopston A.F.C) receiving Fair Play Award from Mr T Hancock Chairman W.W.F.A in 1992. On his left is Mr Bob Waygood.

Ragged School A.F.C Captain Paul James receiving the West Wales Cup from former Evening Post Editor Mr Nick Carter. Vetch Field April 1993.

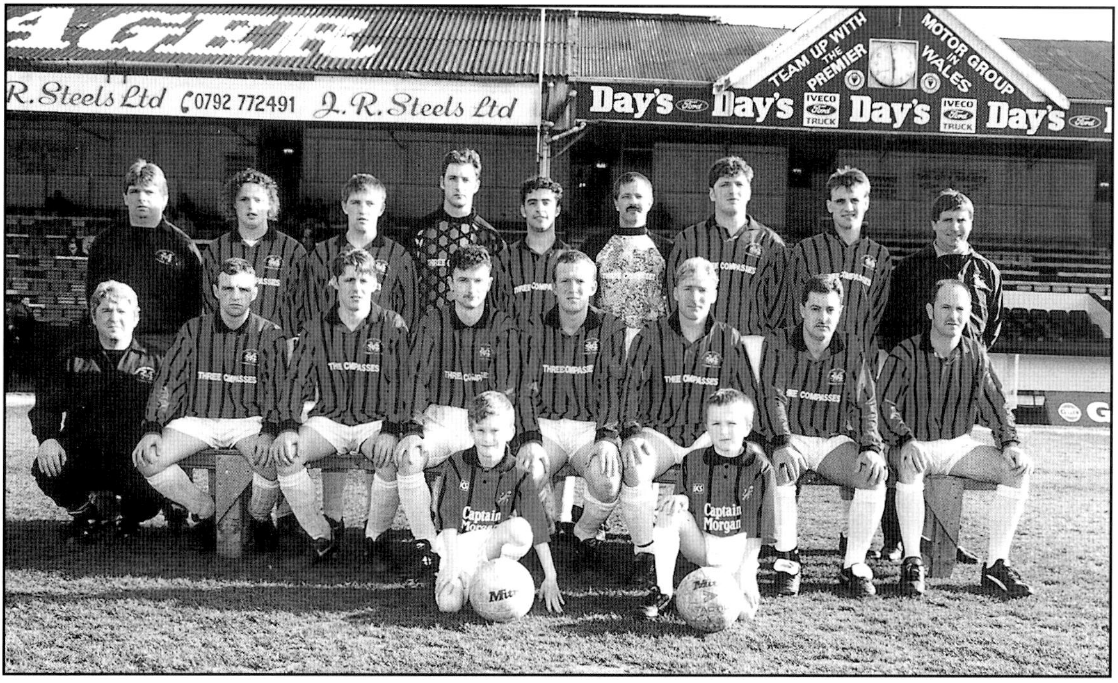

Maltsters Sports A.F.C. Senior Cup Winner 1996-97.
Back (L-R) : A.Norman, P.Brice, M.Johnston, J.Clark, M.Evans, S.Lewis, S.Jones, A.Bowden, G.Hammett.
Front (L-R): L.Donovan, S.Rees, K.Morris, P.Mathews, J.Cadogan, G.Lloyd, A.Davies, C.Bevan.
Mascots: M.Newcombe, J.Mathews.

Port Tennant Colts, Open Cup Final 1992-93
Back (L-R): V.Davies, J.Wright, A.Coles, B.Morgan, I.Midwinter, T.Fender, B.Bidder, B.Connors, A.Naaif, N.Copp, J.Ron.
Front (L-R): M.Ron, N.Lloyd, N.Lewis, G.Dicataldo, N.Dalling,C.Davies.

West End celebrate their W.W.F.A Cup win 1997-98.

St Josephs A.F.C, Swansea League Second Division Champions 1993-94
Back (L-R): Dennis Thomas (Manager), Mark Oliver, Steve Ogle, Jason Evans, Simon Poole, Sean Coughlan, Paul Kavanagh, Mark Evans, Terry Smith.
Front (L-R): Damien Saunders, Paul Cahill, Paul Thomas, Brian Merrighan, Martyn Lewis, Paul Speakman.

Ragged School – Open Cup Winners 1997-98.
Back (L-R) : L.Griffin, B.Dilulio, I.Midwinter, A.Evans, J.Kabia, M.Evans, J.Cornelius.
Front (L-R) : S.Finselbach, I.Lynch, P.Clark, A.Evans, N.Jones, G.Dicataldo, J.Ash.

Brunswick United
Open Cup Runners – Up 1997-98.

Murton Rovers A.F.C
Back (L-R):P.Woodworth, R.Barrett, K.Bowen, J.Jones, W.Froggatt, I.Kennedy, M.Lyle.
Front (L-R):M.Slee, P.Milligan, G.Murphy, Steve Porter, Stuart Porter, T.Desmond.

Naval and Military A.F.C
Back (L-R): B.Mylan, A.Williams, K. Fitzgerald, D.Owens, W.Hurlow, T.Emery, H.Goodridge.
Front (L-R): C.Hurlow, S. Godfrey, L.Williams, J.Quinn, J.Keaveny, A.Davies, D.Phillips.

Brynawel A.F.C
Back (L-R):S.Rees (Referee), R.Hurford, E.Hurford, D.Jones, R.Hurford, S.Davey, M.Miles, D.Rees.
Front (L-R):K.Alexander, R.McClean, D.Mason, L.Thomson, W.Rees, P.Hurford.

Cwmfelin Social A.F.C
Back (L-R):G.Grey, L.Beddins, M.Kennedy, W.Truby, D.Kent, B.Williams, S.Job, S.Broomsfield, S.Heneberry.
Front (L-R):C.Morgan, D.Grove, A.March, I.Booth, M.Lewis.

Plough Colts A.F.C
Back (L-R):L.Coates, R.Parkhouse, S.Popham, D.Lewis, S.Dean, S.Robbins.
Front (L-R):D.Morgan, B.Trotman, J.Brereton, P.Dempster, C.Henley.

Manselton United
Back:W.Davies, D.McQueen, S.Trick, M.Trick, A.Taylor, D.Rigler
Front:P.Davies, A.Jones, D.Jenkins, J. Kiley, A.Thomas, P.Mattews.

SWANSEA REFEREES' SOCIETY.

The Swansea Referee's Association, later to be known as the Swansea Referees' Society, was founded in 1932. Its aims were to promote refereeing and to safeguard the interests of Referees.

The first meetings were held at the Methodist Church in the Hafod, Swansea, with prominent Secretaries being Mr. Charles Mogridge, Mr. Bob Cole, Mr. Ron West, Mr. Jack Jones and Mr. Reg John. Each served with distinction and set the standards for future administrations.

In the early years, the Society was fortunate to have as members, Mr. Bill Gow (Ex Football League and Football Combination), Mr. Bud Fuller (Southern League) and also Mr. Jim Furlong, Mr. Cyril Morris and Mr. Dennis White.

At one stage, the Swansea Referees' Society had no less than six members on the Football League list. John Gow and the late Tommy Reynolds were on the Referees list, John G. P. Davies was on the Supplementary Referees list and all three of these referees were F. I. F. A. and U. E. F. A. "A List" Appointed Referees. George Taylor, Rhydian Harris and Brian Cox were on the linesman's list of Football League.

In recent years, Society members' John Holohan and John Ashman, Officiated on the Football League and John Holohan was appointed to U. E. F. A.'s Referees List with John Ashman being appointed to F. I. F. A.'s Referees List. Currently we have the Referees' Society represented on F. I. F. A.'s Referees List by Simon Jones, and on F. I. F. A.'s Assistant Referees List by Kerry Morgan. On the League of Wales Referees List we have Neil Morgan, John Collins, Mark Whitby and Simon Jones.

On 21st June 1986, the Society was honoured, when it hosted the 68th Annual Conference of the Referees Association. The Headquarters of the Conference was the Dragon Hotel, Swansea, with the Conference being held at the Brangwyn Hall, Swansea. The then Lord Mayor of Swansea, Mrs. Lillian Hopkins Officially opened the conference and was Guest of Honour at the Dinner which followed. Delegates from all parts of England, Northern Ireland and Wales represented their own particular Societies at the conference, which was presided over by Mr. Peter N. Willis, who was an F. A. Cup Final Referee. Swansea was represented by our Chairman Mr. Ken Lewis and the Secretary was Mr. D. J. Davies, both of whom were also responsible for the organisation of this Conference.

Also in 1986, the bond between the Swansea Senior League and the Swansea Referees' Society was strengthened when the League allowed a non-active referee from the Society, to sit on the League's Council and have full voting powers. This was a tremendous gesture by the League and it gave the opportunity for our nominated representative Mr. Terry East to speak on matters that concerned Society

Commitee and wives at Swansea Referees Dinner Dance at Dolphin Hotel

members and also allowed him to report back to the Society, on items raised at Council meetings which were relevant to refereeing.

The 60th Anniversary of the Referees' Society, was celebrated at the Fforest Hotel, Fforestfach, Swansea on 2nd October 1992. Present were President Mr. Bob Waygood, and Life Members Mr. Cyril Morris, Mr. Reg John and Mr. John Gow. Also present were Mr. Eddie Oliver (Secretary of Pembroke F. A.) and Mr. Alan Evans (Secretary of the Football Association of Wales).

Over the years, the Society has held many Dinner and Dance's with invited guests. Pictured below is one such event which took place at the Dolphin Hotel, Swansea. The picture includes such names as Ivor Allchurch, Ray Daniels, Gordon Daniels (Swansea Town Secretary), Bill Edwards. Tom Reynolds, D. G. Evans, Reg John, George Taylor, Jim Helps, Denzil Jones, John Dempster, Cyril Morris and Vince Frendo.

The Society has been very fortunate over the years to have many members who have given not only their time but also their expertise so that new referees entering the Society can call upon a wealth of experience when encountering a problem.

One of the most influential members in recent years has been the current West Wales Referees Officer Mr. John Gow. His support and knowledge of refereeing gained during his years of refereeing on the Football League, has allowed many young referees the opportunity to achieve their ambitions. For their achievements in refereeing, both Mr. John Gow and his late Father Mr. Bill Gow were, at separate times awarded with the Meritorious and Long Service Award, with Mr. John Gow receiving his award in 1961.

There has always been a close co-operation between the Swansea Referees' Society and the Swansea Senior Football League, culminating with the Society donating a Colin Ashford Memorial Award. The recipient is nominated by Society members and a Shield is presented annually at the Society's A. G. M. by Miss Simone Ashford (daughter of Mr. Colin Ashford) to a person associated with the League, for their outstanding service, commitment and co-operation with Match Officials. The first two recipients being Mr. Bryn Bidder (Port Tennant Colts) and Mr. Steve Beasley (Ragged School).

In recent times the Society has had many stalwarts at the helm, serving as Chairman, Secretary or as Officers. Men, such as Roger Upward, D. J. Davies, Terry East, John Holohan, Paul Matthews, Ken Lewis, John Collins, Tony Glacken, John Ashman, Dai Kennedy, D. T. Rees, Colin Clement, Simon Jones, Mark Whitby, Neil Smith, Steve Jones, Dave Allen, Huw Rees and Ken Wright who has served the Society for over 35 years.

At present, the Society's monthly meetings are held at the Coopers Arms in Plasmarl on the last Monday of each month during the Football Season. Guest speakers this year have included John Deakin (League of Wales Appointments Officer), Stewart Davies (Swansea Rugby Captain), Robert Davies (International Rugby Referee), Terry Smith (First Aid and Sports Injuries) and Mr. Keith Cooper (F. A. W. Referee Officer).

The Society competes annually in the Referee Association's 5-a-side Football Competition and Quiz. This has been won on a number of occasions by the Swansea Referees' Society over the years. The Society also holds a Christmas get together with a meal and disco for the Society members and their wives and girlfriends.

The current membership of our Society stands at around 35 members, (including two young female referees), out of a total of 65 West Wales registered referees in Swansea, indicating that our Society is happily moving with the times.

SWANSEA REFEREES' SOCIETY 1999 - 2000

J.Ashman K.Elsey D.Rees L.James H.Rees (Assistant Secretary) B.Bourne T.Drean C.Checketts

J.Passmore V.Nedin D.John C.Last S.R.Jones P.Thomas D.Howard T.East J.Holohan

D.Allen (Vice Chairman) C.Clement D.Kennedy K.Wright M.Whitby (Chairman) R.John J.Davies N.Smith (Secretary)

Gathering at the Llewellyn Hall, Y.M.C.A, for Swansea Referees Society quiz on the laws of the game. Early 1960's.
Included in the group are Referees, Messrs. J.Allen, R.John, T.Reynolds, C.Morris, J.Helps, B.Nelson, Together with representatives from Brunswick and Kilvey Clubs.

Our administrators at present are:-

President:- Mr. Bob Waygood

Chairman:- Mr. Mark Whitby

Secretary:- Mr. Neil Smith

Treasurer:- Mr. John Ashman

Supplies Officer:- Mr. Steve Jones

Life Members:- Mr. John Gow
Mr. Reg John
Mr. Cyril Morris.

The Swansea Referees' Society and the Swansea Football League have always enjoyed close association from their different perspectives. Both have played their part and have allowed many thousands of players to play local football safely, under the Rules of Association Football.

The Swansea Referees' Society congratulates the Swansea Senior League on its 100 Years of local football. It is a tremendous achievement and one in which the League should be extremely proud.

Swansea Registered Referees

Dave Allen
Tony Allender
Andrew Batchelor
Michael Birt
Brian Bourne
Chris Checketts
Colin Clement
John Collins
Jason Copp
Steven Copp
David J. Davies
Philip Davies
Owen Dowdeswell
Tim Drean
Kevin Elsey
Nigel Evans
Ray Evans
Steven Evans
Paul Flavell
Robert Frost
Anthony E. Glacken
Robert Godfrey
Haydn Griffiths
David Grimsley
Adrian Hartley
Nigel Hill
John Holohan
Clive Hopkins
Darryl Howard
Lee James
Paul Jenkins
Dean John
John Jones
Simon Jones
Steven R. Jones
David Kennedy
Ken Lewis
Phil McIntyre
Kerry Morgan
Elizabeth Nedin
Richard Neville
Robert Otten
Malcolm Owen
David T. Rees
Huw Rees
Richard Regan
Nigel Richards
Ciro Ruggierio
Neil Smith
Clive Steward
Chris Stilwell
Colin Suttie
Nigel Thorne
Peter Thomas
Mark Whitby
David Wyn Williams
Richard J. Williams
Ken Wright

SWANSEA SENIOR ASSOCIATION FOOTBALL LEAGUE ANNUAL SIX A SIDE COMPETITION.

It was during the 1962-63 season that the idea of the league holding a six a side competition was first muted. Many meetings were then held to discuss its formation and also to formulate the rules of such a competition.

Presentation of new six-a-side trophy to the league by Mr Cliff Curvis, to League Chairman Mr George Peters, in April 1964.

At a special meeting of the League Council on the 17th April 1963, Mr. Cliff Curvis, on behalf of his brother Brian and himself, presented a cup to the League in memory of their late father. This cup was to be played for annually, as the Swansea Senior League six a side competition.

The first competition was held on Saturday, 27th April 1963, it took place at the Ashleigh Road playing fields. Forty five teams would enter and the competition was a resounding success. Being a new venture, many fancied teams, not being used to this type of football, fell by the wayside. Eventually after five rounds and some very exciting competition, Winch Wen and Port Tennant Stars competed in the final.

Port Tennant were to prove no match for a very young and skillful Winch Wen side, they eventually became the very first winners of the six a side trophy, beating the Stars by 4 goals to nil.

The star of this first successful competition was undoubtedly John Watkins, who would go on to become a very fine local and Welsh League player.

Teams:-
Winch Wen:
C. Mogridge, B. Hughes, J. Watkins, J. Slattery, R. Jones, G. Harris, J. Jones, C. Rees.

Port Tennant Stars:
T. Maunders, A. Maunders, C. Thomas, J. Poole, G. Lewis, T. Barratt, H. Matthews, R. Davies.

The Curvis brothers presented the trophy, and it brought to a close a memorable competition. It was noted in the League minutes of May 1963, that many clubs had written in to congratulate the League on its organisation of this new venture. The letters also expressed the hope that this competition would be the forerunner of many more such events.

The six a side competition continued for many years, and was always considered a light relief from the slog of league and cup competitions. Many fine sides would win the competition over the years and it was always considered a feast of football.

Then due to various reasons the competition lost its appeal. Perhaps it was as a result of some clubs being involved in so many vital league and cup games. Another reason given was that a lot of clubs didn't consider it worth the effort to perhaps turn up and lose in the first round. Whatever the reasons, the competition finally terminated in season 1980-81.

Over the years many people have expressed their regrets over the termination of this competition. Perhaps the League should have taken on board as to the best time to hold such a tournament. A competition like this needs good weather, players can be hanging around between matches, if the weather is cold and wet, then it can be uncomfortable. Perhaps a pre-season competition could have been the answer, clubs and players could have used it as a very useful warm up.

To make it worthwhile for players to make the effort, perhaps a Plate competition could be introduced whereby, first round losers, could then take part in a subsidiary competition. Why not play it on the same day as the Charity Shield final? It could be played on the all weather pitches at the Morfa, and then the finals just prior to the Shield final when there is a big crowd on hand.

Any choices are worth the consideration to get this trophy underway again, the Cup was given in good faith, in memory of a good man who did so much for local sport. Come on the Swansea Senior League - give it a try.

	WINNERS	RUNNERS UP
1962-63	Winch Wen	Port Tennant Stars
1963-64	Swansea Town 'A'	Portmead
1964-65	West End	North End
1965-66	North End	Hafod Brotherhood
1966-67	Rockspur	Swansea Boys Club
1967-68	West End	United
1968-69	Port Tennant Stars	Tower
1969-70	Port Tennant Colts	Swansea Boys Club
1970-71	No Competition	
1971-72	St. Joseph's	Rum Rangers
1972-73	United	Farmers
1973-74	Hafod Brotherhood	Waun Wen
1974-75	BSC (Cwm Press)	West End
1975-76	Bonymaen Colts	Swansea Boys Club
1976-77	West End	Swansea Boys Club
1977-78	West End	St. Joseph's
1978-79	No Competition	
1979-80	No Competition	
1980-81	Portmead	Port Tennant Colts

Six –a –Side Competition.
Three sides from the early six-a-side competition.

Top: Gwent B.C
Middle: Murton Rovers
Bottom: Tower

ONE HUNDRED YEARS

One Hundred Years - it has come and gone.

Like the proverbial harassed housewife at the end of a busy day would say "where has the time gone - the day has flown".

There is no shadow of a doubt that local football has provided the biggest sporting outlet for the people of Swansea. It is to their credit that for the past 100 years, the Swansea Senior Association Football League, has provided organised league and cup football.

Other Leagues in the area have also played a part in local football. Between the two world wars, the Swansea Sunday Schools League and the Swansea Gwalia League were very strong organisations. With the amalgamation of the Gwalia League and the Swansea Senior League after the second world war, and then the demise of the Sunday Schools League at roughly the same time, has meant that the Swansea Senior League would be the only one to survive.

The League has, as stated many times in this history, been fortunate to be served over the years by many fine administrators. In saying this, the League must also share the praise with the many fine club administrators and officials. Those people who come every match day, never mind how foul the weather, will ensure that their clubs will provide football for their players. These are the unsung heroes of the League, and without these officials, clubs would not survive. Whereas the loyalty of a lot of players can be seriously questioned, there can be no such questioning of a lot of club officials who have given many, many years to the game.

When one mentions names there is always a chance that someone will be offended, and taking this on board, many such names would come readily to hand. Bryn Bidder at Port Tennant Colts is an obvious choice, Bryn has been at the helm of Crymlyn Burrows B. C. and the Colts for over fifty years. Whilst the name of Billy Johns will always be synonymous with Mumbles Rangers, and quite rightly so, anyone going to the Mumbles to play since the fifties will always have some association with Fred Clements. A lovely man with time for everyone, he has also been a great servant to football in the west of the city.

Who could ever forget going to Ashleigh Road and seeing the Hafod Brotherhood duo of Jack Jones and Cyril Edwards, for years displaying the drive and devotion to their club, whilst the same would apply to Jimmy McIntee for his beloved St. Joseph's. Both these clubs are in a fortunate position that this passion can be carried on by such people as Billy Davies at the Hafod, and the Smith brothers at the Saints. Here again all three being loyal serving clubmen.

Ashleigh Road during the fifties, sixties and seventies, was undoubtedly a great place to be on a Saturday. It had a buzz about it and would be massed with supporters. One of the biggest battles at Ashleigh Road during these years was trying to obtain a permit to play on Pitch 9, as this was the biggest and best of the pitches and every club wanted to play there. With that said, it would seem that Hafod Brotherhood always had something on the Parks Department, so readily did they get allocated this pitch.

On the times that North End would obtain the pitch, who would ever forget that massive tarpaulin sheet that their many supporters would extend and hold over them to keep off the driving rain sweeping across from The Mumbles. They were a fanatical bunch and great company. Here again the club have been lucky to have had such servants as the Barry brothers. Whilst talking of brothers, the input and dedication of the three Thomas brothers, Roy, Tommy and Brian, is without doubt immense. The Thomas boys, together with the loveable Ivor Williams, have been synonymous with the North End club for many years.

There have been many such associations of officials and clubs, George Morgan and Stepney, Dai Maddick and Winch Wen, W. G. Cole, Mal Bailey and Ernie Morgan with Ragged School, and Albert Mainwaring with Port Tennant Stars. In some cases families became synonymous with clubs, the Marles family with Rockspur, the Days with Welsh Juniors and in more recent days, the Morgan family at the Heathcliff.

The list is endless, others who come to mind would include Glyn Bidder who gave his all for Cwmfelin Press, John Cooze would do the same for Cwm Albion. Len Davies and John Lewis were long associated with Waun Wen, whilst the hard work put in by Jack McGillvary at Brunswick has been maintained by the unstinting efforts of Mike Paddison. Perhaps one of the longest serving officials of the present day clubs is Alex Milne, who was the founder member of the Unifloc United team. The team was based in Morriston and all the players at the time worked in the Unifloc factory. After several seasons the club changed its name to Bishopston A. F. C., this coming about when they acquired a pitch in Pwll-Du-Lane. Alex proudly relates that in 1999 they realised their one remaining ambition when they actually reached a Swansea League cup final after 37 years in the League.

Three others who must be mentioned in this category are Arthur Harris, Edwin Harris and Bernard Lee, all three over the years have given outstanding service to their clubs. Both Arthur and Edwin were of the same mould, they gave their all for the Tower and Dillwyn clubs and they were both fiercely competitive in everything they did. Both were loveable characters, who would have their critics and even though Arthur is sadly gone, one is sure that they would both agree that they could work the odd scam or ten.

Bernard Lee was another who put in so much for his club. He worked hard at the Swansea Boys Club and built a really first class side. A quiet man, Bernard had time for everyone, even when in poor health he continued to support and follow his Boys Club team.

These names are sure to bring back memories to a lot of people, but as previously stated, to name names can be a danger, someone is sure to come up with people who have also dedicated time and passion to their clubs. The League realises this and would like to make it perfectly clear that they not only recognise the people mentioned, but also realise the part that every official, at every club, has played in the League's history.

Whilst the Swansea League readily and heartily acknowledge the players, officials and supporters of clubs, it must also place on record the outstanding contribution made by its officers and councillors over the years. This history of the League has recognised its officers and administrators at some point, but would also stress the importance of the role that the Executive Council has played. The Council, made up of life members, vice presidents and elected members, play a very important part in the running of the League.

These members are unpaid, travel at their own expense to various meetings at various venues and spend many hours of their free time at these meetings. It is a thankless task and one that should receive more recognition than it does. Many is the moan of the decisions of League Council but overall their input is an immense contribution to the running of the League.

Other players who play a big part in this League are the West Wales F. A. and the Swansea Referees Society. The League have been affiliated to the West Wales F. A. since the ruling body was set up in 1922, and have always worked in close harmony with the Association. It is significant that the three main administrators of the West Wales F. A., Messrs. R. Waygood, J. Davies and J. Gow, are all ex referees, all three gave many years of service to the Swansea League. All three put in a tremendous amount of work and are all fully supportive of the League's effort to promote local football.

As we go into a new century, the League will aim to continue to provide a high standard of football for the people of Swansea. It is the biggest sporting outlet in the area and the League now boasts of 190 clubs with over 4,500 registered players. Add to this the number of officials and supporters and you realise that the local soccer fraternity is a huge percentage of the population of the City.

This history closes quoting the 1974 British Lions captain Willie John McBride, who told his touring party: "It's been great to travel with you". It certainly has, and here's to the next 100 years.

DAVID EVANS. Sports Editor, South Wales Evening Post.

IT SEEMS like only yesterday . . . but in fact it is more than 30 years since I first came into contact with the Swansea Senior League.

It was incumbent on the junior sports reporter of the Evening Post in those days to telephone round the various club secretaries for results and scorers of that weekend's matches. Time consuming stuff, but I wouldn't have missed it for the world.

It provided the perfect opportunity to start to learn the basic skills of journalism and also made you aware that sport - and this applies to all levels - invariably involves meeting some good people.

When I first started doing the rounds in those long gone pre-Soccer Extra days, North End and Hafod Brotherhood were in their prime. Then along came the famous Swansea Boys Club side which swept through the league with promotion after promotion and championship after championship followed by West End and the East Side giants, the Stars and the Colts.

Colin Ashford became one of the hardest-working league secretaries I have come across in any sport and there were plenty of club officials like Frank Davies, Bryn Bidder and Barry Griffiths ready and willing to offer their assistance as long as you got their team in the headlines. There were characters on the field like Charlie Leyshon and Cyril Hartson (his son isn't a bad player either) and top referees like John Gow and Tom Reynolds.

But although time moves on and memories fade, the strong links between the League and the Evening Post remain and perhaps have grown even stronger.

I remember the time when we came up with the idea of producing a four-page pull-out covering the length and breadth of our circulation area. It was down to me to pull the thing together, a major operation featuring a report on all the matches in the top divisions with teams, referees name etc.

My first call was to Colin Ashford. I explained what was required and there was silence. After a pause of several seconds Colin said "Leave it to me." Within the hour Colin was back on the phone. "Can't see many problems with that," he said, and from that point I knew that Soccer Extra would become a reality, and it remains to this day an integral part of the Evening Post's success.

By 8.30 every Monday morning Colin would have dropped off at our Adelaide Street main office a bulging envelope containing hand written reports on every match played in the top three divisions of the Saturday league, a round up of the lower divisions and the equivalent from the Sunday League. No faxes, e-mails or the like in those days, just good old fashioned pen and paper.

Latterly it has been the reliable Stuart McDonald who has been giving up much of his weekend to ensure that local soccer - and the Swansea Senior League in particular - gets the recognition it deserves.

I am sure that whoever follows me at the Evening Post in future years will ensure that this link is maintained.

Happy Birthday.

WEST WALES FOOTBALL ASSOCIATION

There are moments in everyone's life when one feels a deep sense of pride, either with personal achievements or associations with worthwhile organisations. I am sure that everyone connected with the Swansea Senior and Sunday A. F. L. feels that sense of pride as the League celebrates its Centenary.

I have been associated with the League for nearly 40 years. My first recollection was as a Referee in 1962, but by 1965 had returned to playing. I played for a few Clubs, but in the main it was RTB Landore. In 1972 it was Refereeing again until 1977 when I was appointed the assistant Secretary of the West Wales Football Association and in 1978 became their Secretary.

Since my association with the League, I have become aware of the many great traditions which have been established, the many servants who have contributed to the success of the League. Also, the thousands of players who play every weekend to probably the highest standards in grass roots football in Wales, with many in past years being 'scouted' by the old 'Football League'. And not forgetting the Referees where many have reached the highest standards through having a good grounding within the League.

The League with its 17 Divisions is most certainly the largest in Wales and could very well be the largest League in the United Kingdom.

Much success has been achieved throughout their history with representative teams having won many Inter-League Competitions and Clubs winning many honours in Area Association and National Competitions. Thus highlighting the strength of the Clubs who participate in the League.

I am delighted to have been asked to make a contribution to this Centenary Publication outlining the History of the League, and wish them every success over the next 100 years.

Bob Waygood
Hon General Secretary.

Geoff Wheel.

It is a great honour and a pleasure to have been asked to make a contribution to this compilation of the history of the Swansea Senior Football League. I consider it a privilege indeed to have been asked, and I am quite sure that there are many sportsmen in the area who are far more qualified than myself to do so.

I owe a great debt to the League and in particular Port Tennant Colts and Mr. Bryn Bidder, along with his colleagues and my friends for starting me out on my sporting career, albeit that I ended up playing a game with the wrong shaped ball.

It is the time and effort and the sheer enthusiasm that these people who encourage and administer sport at local level across the City which always astounds me. It is something we should all be very grateful for in our respective communities, for providing young people with the opportunity to share in the sporting spirit and foster friendships which will remain for the rest of their lives.

My years spent playing with the Colts were extremely happy ones, playing for the under 15's to the under 18's and then in to the reserve side for a spell, before moving on to rugby football at the late age of nineteen.

I can't help feeling that when I first walked on to Lansdowne Road to play my first rugby international against Ireland, that part of my Senior League football grounding, experience and support was with me. It provided me with the confidence that all sportsmen need when faced with their greatest challenge.

My very best wishes to this history being compiled and I trust that the Swansea Senior League will continue to successfully grow and develop into the new millennium.

Geoff Wheel.

John Gow. (Former League, Football League and F. I. F. A. Referee)

It was a fine April Saturday afternoon in 1952 that I started my career as a referee. A late appointment to officiate at Ashleigh Road (tin sheds were the dressing rooms) in a match Hafod Brotherhood. v Plasmarl in the 1st Division of the Senior League. The fee was 7s 6p. plus expenses. What could you buy for that money in those days? Two seats at the cinema, box of chocolates for the girl friend and still have change.

When I look back at that match, two things stand out, how on earth did I receive such an appointment as a first match, and also, it made me realise that club linesmen were slightly biased to say the least. From that day to the end of my career, club linesmen were told only to tell me when the ball was out of play. Any mistakes, there have been many, were to be my own.

The next few seasons saw the standard of matches allocated to me gradually increase in importance. At the end of season 1953-54 I was awarded my Class B. National Service beckoned. By the time two years had elapsed, I had progressed to a Class A referee and moved to Birmingham where I remained for ten years.

During that time I had attained Football League status as a referee. Whilst living in Birmingham I maintained my connection with the Senior League and the F. A. W. by officiating during my vacations in Swansea. One of my prized mementoes is the silver whistle presented to me by the League in 1967.

For the season 1966-67 my wife and I were back in Swansea and I was officiating on a regular basis in the Senior League when not officiating in the Football League. My first game in that season was at Cwm Level and I can remember the Cwm Albion captain asking me if this was my first game in the League. I replied yes. Within ten minutes of the start of the game, one player was sent off for kicking an opponent. I can assure you all he was most surprised.

Throughout the rest of my career I always enjoyed my games in the Senior League. In the space of five days, I officiated at Highbury (55,000) on the Saturday, on the Monday at Velindre (10 men and a dog), and on the Wednesday at Real Madrid before 100,000 spectators. All these matches had one thing in common, the Laws of the Game were the same.

I have been fortunate to officiate at Cup Finals, Senior Cups, 6 a side tournaments and three F. A.W. Senior Cup Finals.

I have served under three League Secretaries, Bryn Williams, Walter Quick and Colin Ashford. They gave me the encouragement that any new referee needs in his career, they were also prepared to release me at short notice to officiate at Football League level after I had accepted a Senior League appointment.

Refereeing involves long periods away from home, travelling all over the country. I was fortunate to be friendly with your late President George Jones, who during the last ten years of my career travelled to every match that I officiated. We were both proud to be associated with the Senior League and many Club officials in the Football League were fully aware of the existence of the Senior League.

The Senior League has been responsible for the development and the advancement of many referees since its inauguration. There is no doubt in my mind that the standard of football is not only the best, but throughout its divisions it is extremely competitive.

What has changed in recent years is the attitude of players to the referee, this mirrors society's reluctance to authority. Spectator numbers have become smaller but are more verbal and abusive on the touchline.

I wish the League every success in the future.

Frank Davies (Life Member of the W. W. F. A., Ex-Secretary of the W. W. F. A. 1967-1974).

I was delighted to be asked to recall my years with my involvement in local football, this involvement and love affair with game locally, is now over sixty years. My first introduction to football was as a schoolboy, playing for the Cadle School at thirteen, where incidentally my best pal and team mate was George Morgan. We both then progressed to play for St. Peters in the old Gwalia League.

I first became involved with the West Wales F. A. in 1950, I was approached by Mr. Bryn Williams (Swansea Senior League Sec.) and Mr. Ossie Rees, to ask whether I would be prepared to assist Mr. Rees, prior to him becoming Secretary of the Association in 1954. I was elected to West Wales F. A. council representing Fforestfach as a Section A club. In 1956 I became Assistant Secretary of the Association, a position I held until taking over as Secretary in 1967.

I recall many great people of this era, men who had stature in the local game. One such man was Mr. S. B. Williams, often regarded as the foundation of the West Wales F. A. in those days, a great man and a great Secretary. Other great characters who come readily to mind were, A. R. Price, C. H. Marles, T. J. Richards, G. J. McIntyre, E. G. Williams and not forgetting Mr. Bryn Williams, he was the corner stone of the Swansea League.

Then you had referees who were great characters, such men as G. Peters, R. L. Cole, J. J. Edwards, R. W. Fuller, W. J. Gow (Senior), J. D. Jones, R. V. John and C. F. Morris. Their pearls of wisdom, passed on to players before a match were such, "Now lads, I have come to enjoy a game of football, Do not disappoint me", or "You know lads if you have an early bath, then the water will be cold". They were all characters, today's referees don't seem to think the same.

You also had great characters as Secretaries, names that readily come to mind include, Frank Wheatley at Clydach, Bill Pass at Landore, Evan Taylor at Morristion, Johnny Cooze, Arthur Beale, Glyn Cole, Redvers Marles, Edwin Harris, Arthur Harris, Jack Jones, Dai Maddick and Glyn Bidder.

Two other people would play a big part in my footballing life, Bryn Williams, whom I found to be cool, calm and above all, totally honest. The other person is Tom Richards, he like Bryn, was honest and sincere. Colin Ashford was another great administrator, who gave his all to the League.

I wish the Swansea League all the very best for the future, I trust they will go on in style and honest administration, as your predecessors before you would have wished.

ROY LLOYD. (Former Player)
A Stroll through 50 year of Senior League.

Firstly, might I state that this is not about who was the best player or which was the best team. This is simply a list of happy memories of various characters who either played, watched or administered the game during this wonderful period. No person mentioned here will be referred to as the 'The Late', because, although they have passed on, what they left behind remains with us.

My memories started after World War 2 when, if Swansea were playing away, my friends and I would go to Paradise Park or Cwmbrwla to watch the men play. One of these first memories was watching a game between Nelson and Graigola Fuel Works, the Graigola team had come straight from work and were as black as the ace of spades.

I also recall the emergence of the very good Townhill sides at the time, Tower under Arthur Harris and Gwent under Eddie Bryant. Then followed the Hillsborough club with the Edwards brothers, Harry and Hughie, and the Merlin club with the Trick brothers. Another fine Hill club at the time were Rockspur, under the guidance of Mr. Marles. Later on then came the very fine Tower side with the likes of Ray and Ronnie Davies, Dai Landry and Graham Chislett, alongside were the Boys Club who in Bobby Coates and Bobby Grills, had two of the best players at the time. The Boys Club tradition would then be carried on by first Bernard Lee, then by Gethin Roberts and his troops.

Football in Swansea would be a lesser place without the teams from the East Side. Port Tennant Stars held the rein for many years with players such as Les Evans, Bill Ashford, Harry Davies and Ron Ley, this tradition would then be carried on by the likes of Hubert Mathews, Cyril Thomas and Alan Maunders. Talking of Ron Ley, many opponents reckoned his legs could reach each touchline without moving, such was his stature. Still in the East Side, there was the very strong Dockers side, just up the road then was the Kilvey team, with the likes of John Laurie, Keith Huntley and Davo Davies, were more than a match for anyone. Mention must be made of Bryn Bidder with Port Tennant Colts, he does deserve a special mention. Many a useful player has changed in the dressing rooms at Maesteg Park, when you went up the steps there you were in for a battle. Long may it remain so.

I remember Mumbles Baptist with the likes of Ben Hoppe, Don John and John Budge, whilst Brunswick had the James brothers, Roy, Freddie and Albert. North End were one of my favourites, wonderfully served by the Barry brothers, whilst the Thomas brothers Roy, Tommy and Brian, have given their all for the club. Can we ever forget also the irreplaceable pair of Ivor Williams and Charles Leyshon. Other clubs that come readily to mind are the Ragged School, Hafod Brotherhood, St. Joseph's, Cwm Albion and Waun Wen, all great clubs that have given lads the opportunity to play the game. The list is endless, Dillwyn with Edwin Harris, Plasmarl, Cwmfelin Press and Gors United with Lenny John, Billy Rees and Elwyn Evans were a strong outfit.

Swansea Town regularly competed in the League and people like Abe Freedman, the Chairman, and Harry Griffiths, later to be the Manager, knew almost everyone in the league, a relationship which is sadly missed now. Morriston had the Richards brothers, Unit Colts/United were very strong, and also had Billy Abrahamson who thought he was the original Peter Pan. Alexandra, Crofty, Welsh Juniors, I could go on and on.

So when all you young men go out on a Saturday, just think what you represent, before you start, look up and around and say a little thank you. Please play with pride.

This memory is dedicated to the hundreds of players and officials who have not been mentioned.

Jack Thomas (Garden Village - Memories of early days).

Football, according to older colleagues, was first played in Garden Village about the year 1921-22, this was just after the completion of the building of the village after the world war one, the later development began around 1938.

When it was realised that a team could be started in the village, it was decided to form a committee to oversee the development. It is said that the first Chairman was a Mr. Jack Davies, his fellow members included Mr. Mark Gray (who's great grandson plays for the club today), Messrs. Jack and Will Griffiths, Dick Lewis (Yankee), Dick Thomas and Jack Thomas. This committee, along with the enthusiastic players, worked hard to prepare a playing area. The land for the pitch was leased from the Duke of Beauforts Estate Agents for one shilling (5 pence) per year.

It is believed the club joined the Swansea and District League in 1922-23 season and played against clubs in the Swansea, Upper Swansea Valley and the Neath area. Travelling to away matches always caused problems, there were no cars to travel in and a bus was a luxury. It was sometimes possible to hire a 'charabanc', when this happened all the kids were allowed on to fill the bus. On occasions, if you were lucky, a coal lorry would take the village teams away, this would be after it had been given a brush down to get rid of the coal dust. For home games, visiting sides would be invited to a committee mans or players homes to enable them to change. Later a shed became available, 'showers' were two tin baths, if you were last to wash it would be a mud bath. How times have changed.

Every player had to pay weekly subs to the club treasurer, usually 3 old pennies per week, if these subs were not paid by the Friday evening, there was no game for you on the Saturday. The subs had to be collected so that the referee could have his match fee and expenses, usually about two shillings or half a crown (10 to 12½ pence).

It was in the thirties that the Garden Village side joined the newly formed Gwalia League, then in season 1938-39, the club withdrew from the Swansea League to join the Carmarthenshire League, where they still play to this day. Those early years with the Swansea and District League will always be remembered with fondness, they were the formative years for a club which has gone from strength to strength to achieve its present status.

A TRIBUTE TO COLIN ASHFORD

Colin J Ashford
Hon.Sec. Swansea Senior League. 1967 – 1996.

When the late Walter Quick resigned as Secretary of the Swansea Senior League in 1968, to take up a coaching appointment with the West Wales F. A. there was great speculation as to who in the League set-up would replace him. The post was subsequently advertised and when the appointment of Colin Ashford was announced, people asked "Colin who?" Little did they realise then, that he would become one of the most influential figures in local football. The Swansea Senior League was to become his passion, and some would say that apart from his family, it was his life. Colin was a devoted family man, and with the support of his wife Jean and daughter Simone, he virtually ran the show single-handed until his untimely death in June 1996.

Colin was educated at Dynevor Secondary School. In his youth he was a very keen rugby player, and he was also a top class cyclist, being a member of the Swansea Wheelers C. C. On leaving school he took up an appointment with the then British Electricity Authority as a wages clerk, then moving on with the same company to work at Hinkley Point Power Station in Somerset, before returning to the local authority. Colin then accepted the position of Administration Officer with B. P. Chemicals at their Baglan Bay works, a position he held until his retirement in 1993.

On his appointment in 1968, with the Swansea Senior League, Colin quickly got to grips with the position. He imposed his own style and was quick to show Council that he was more than capable of taking the League on to further progress. Within months he was into his stride and running the show single-handedly, which was the way that Colin liked to do things. He proved himself more than a match for any outside body who attempted to take liberties or bring in unfair legislation. Many was the time that such people had their fingers burnt when dealing with him in such situations.

In 1968, Sunday football was getting under way. At the time perhaps one would describe it as a little shambolic, but it was Colin's desire to bring all local Sunday Football under the umbrella of the Swansea Senior League so that it would become more organised. At the end of the 1968-69 season, the West Wales F. A. agreed that the Swansea Senior League could organise Sunday football within the Swansea District. In July 1970, it was agreed that the Swansea Senior Sunday League (a subsidiary of the Swansea Senior League) would organise Sunday football and a Division was formed for the 1970-71 season. This again meant more work, but it was Colin's thinking that if Sunday football was to flourish, then it should be under the wing of the Swansea Senior League. Once again he was proved right as we have seen the Sunday League expand from just one division to its present five divisions and subsequent Sunday cups.

Apart from his virtual full time activities with League duties, Colin was also a long serving member of the West Wales F. A., and this service saw him take over as Chairman of the Association during the years 1986-88. He was also heavily involved with the Swansea Referees' Society and was well respected by all referees, assessors and referees administrators.

Colin was always available, and it didn't seem to bother him that people would telephone never mind what time of the day or night. The phone was always red hot, but he had time for everyone's problems. People were always welcome to call at his home whether it be with forms, letters, team sheets or just for advice. Saying that, if you didn't like dogs then it wasn't the place to be. Visitors would be greeted by two of the biggest dogs you would ever see, and you sat there afraid to move. Many is the time that Colin would come before Council and inform them that he hadn't received various correspondence, he could only assume that the dogs had eaten it. Saying this, many believed Colin used this excuse many a time when it suited him, but everyone accepted the dogs and his reasonings.

When Colin suddenly passed away in June 1996, the whole of the local soccer world was in a state of shock. It was a feeling of disbelief and to many, the passing of someone who could never be replaced. It was the end of an era. Someone who had taken the Swansea Senior League to a level that was the envy of most Welsh football. Colin was called many things, when you are successful you get this, autocratic, selfish, self opinionated, you name it and I suppose Colin had been called it. Knowing Colin, he would probably have agreed with them all. He would have had a good laugh and carried on with no resentment whatsoever, he was that kind of man. He was something different, and his passing was not only a tragic loss to the Swansea Senior League, but to all football in general.

LEAGUE AND INTERNATIONAL PLAYERS.

The Swansea Senior League has, during it history, produced many fine teams and players. Some of these players have been fortunate enough to go on and play at a professional level and in some cases to represent their country.

What the League has attempted to do is to produce a list of players who have signed for Football League clubs whilst playing in the Swansea Senior League. The list does not include players who were already on schoolboy or amateur forms with League clubs whilst playing in our League.

One would imagine that there are many more players that could be added to the list, particularly those from the early years, even so, the list that has been recorded does show what fine players this League has produced. Many people would argue that the local City team has never given local players the chance that some have merited. The club, like many other professional clubs, still persists with a policy of bringing in free transfer signings. Most of these players have either 'done the rounds' or have been discarded by clubs as not being up to the grade. Most of these players have subsequently been shown to be no better than players in our local leagues.

Arguments and discussion have always been on going, as to which players would have made it if given the chance. Older people will relate that many players in the early days deserved a break. In more modern times, when one looks at why such players as Len Mathews, John Pope, Alan Maunders, Phil Jones, Donny Smitham, Ernie Phillips, Johnny Jones etc., didn't get a chance, surely lends argument to the lobby that the system is flawed.

Mark Baker	Ragged School	Swansea
Alan Beer	United	Swansea
Sid Clarke	Kilvey	Clapton Orient
John Comley	Hafod Brotherhood	Carlisle
Terry Cotton	Ragged School	Swansea
* Dai Davies	St. Joseph's	Everton
Glen Davies	Ragged School	Swansea
Glyn Davies	Bolton Wanderers	
Kevin Davies	Ragged School	Cardiff
Terry Davies	Hafod Brotherhood	Arsenal
Carl Elsey	Ragged School	Queens Park Rangers
Ken Evans	S. W. Builders	Swansea
* Trevor Ford	Tower United	Swansea
* Steve Gammon	Mumbles Rangers	Cardiff
Gwilym Gimblett	Morriston	Bolton Wanderers
Jeff Griffiths	Sketty Park	Swansea
David Gwyther	South Gower	Swansea
* Billy Harris	Clarence	Middlesborough
Jamie Harris	Mumbles Rangers	Swansea
* Jeff Hopkins	Hafod Brotherhood	Fulham
Eddie Humphreys	Rockspur	Swansea
Keith Huntley	St. Judes	Swansea
* Jack Kelsey	Winch Wen	Arsenal
Tom Kiley		Swansea
Michael Lenihan	Swansea Boys Club	Swansea
Willie Messer	Belgrave	Swansea
Edgar Newell	Fforestfach	Swansea
Donald Payne	Ragged School	Newport County
Dudley Peake	Townhill	Swansea
Don Pearson	St. Judes	Swansea
Anthony Pennock	North End	Hereford
Ray Powell	Morriston	Swansea
Brian Purcell	Waun Wen	Swansea
* Jack Roberts	Highbury	Bolton Wanderers
Len Rowden	Plasmarl	Swansea
* Frank Scrine	Baldwins	Swansea
Clive Slattery	Winch Wen	Swansea
Henry Smale	Hafod Brotherhood	Derby County
Fred Stevens	Hafod Brotherhood	Cardiff
Iorrie Symmons	St. Paul's	Swansea
Wyn Thomas	Consolidated	Halifax
Barry Tucker	Ragged School	Northampton
Billy Wilkins	Hafod Brotherhood	Bolton Wanderers

* Denotes International.

PAST OFFICERS OF THE LEAGUE.

CHAIRMEN:

Mr. Josh Walters.	
Rev. J. Crole.	
Mr. H. Howells.	
Mr. W. J. Sheldon.	
Mr. J. W. Thorpe.	
Major Mullard.	
Mr. Walter Crutchley.	
Mr. Albert Clement.	
Mr. David Jones.	
Mr. D. J. Sambrook.	
Mr. Phil Beynon.	
Mr. J. Patterson.	
Mr. Thomas Ball.	
Mr. Thomas Cole.	
Mr. T. R. Evans.	
Mr. C. H. Harding.	
Mr. Hugh Jones.	
Mr. Bryn Williams.	
Mr. William Parker.	
Mr. C. H. Marles.	1946-48
Mr. G. J. McIntyre.	1948-49
Mr. E. W. Taylor.	1949-50
Mr. D. W. Maddick.	1950-51
Mr. Thomas Day.	1951-52
Mr. J. F. Gabriel.	1952-53
Mr. William Cooze.	1953-54
Mr. T. J. Richards.	1954-56
Mr. Jack Thomas.	1956-58
Mr. D. A. Williams.	1958-60
Mr. A. Beale.	1960-62
Mr. G. Peters.	1962-64
Mr. J. Cohen.	1964-66
Mr. B. Jenkins.	1966-68
Mr. J. E. Budge.	1968-70
Mr. George Jones.	1970-72
Mr. E. Williams.	1972-74
Mr. G. Bidder.	1974-76
Mr. W. A. Harris.	1976-78
Mr. M. Bailey.	1978-80
Mr. C. C. Price.	1980-82
Mr. L. Morgan.	1982-84
Mr. J. D. Morgan.	1984-86
Mr. D. A. White.	1986-88
Mr. D. Arnold.	1988-90
Mr. B. Thomas.	1990-92
Mr. L. Davies.	1992-94
Mr. D. Savage.	1994-96
Mr. N. Tucker.	1996-98
Mr. L. J. Carter.	1998-2000
Mr. S. Hammett.	2000-2002

HON. SECRETARIES:

Mr. Charles Jenkins	1901-18
Mr. J. W. Sparkes	1918-39
Mr. A. R. Price	1939-45
Mr. Bryn Williams	1946-61
Mr. W. Quick	1961-68
Mr. C. J. Ashford	1968-96
Mr. L. S. Evans	1996-

HON. TREASURERS.

Mr. S. B. Williams
Mr. Sam Rees
Mr. Ossie Rees
Mr. E. G. Williams
Mr. A. Conibear
Mr. R. A. Kent.
Mr. S. L. McDonald